Guest-Edited by
PATRIK SCHUMACHER

RETHINKING
ARCHITECTURE'S
AGENDA FOR THE
21ST CENTURY

PARAMETRICISM 2.0

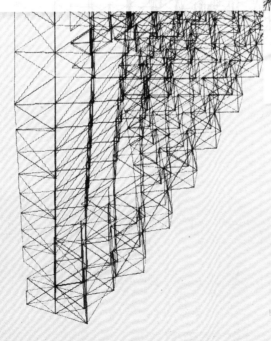

ARCHITECTURAL DESIGN
March/April 2016

Profile
No 240

ISSN 0003-8504
ISBN 978-1118-736166

Editorial Offices
John Wiley & Sons
25 John Street
London WC1N 2BS
UK

T +44 (0)20 8326 3800

Editor
Helen Castle

Managing Editor (Freelance)
Caroline Ellerby

Production Editor
Elizabeth Gongde

Prepress
Artmedia, London

Art Direction + Design
CHK Design:
Christian Küsters
Christos Kontogeorgos

Printed in Italy by Printer
Trento Srl

Journal Customer Services
For ordering information, claims and any enquiry concerning your journal subscription please go to www.wileycustomerhelp .com/ask or contact your nearest office.

Americas
E: cs-journals@wiley.com
T: +1 781 388 8598 or
+1 800 835 6770 (toll free in the USA & Canada)

Europe, Middle East and Africa
E: cs-journals@wiley.com
T: +44 (0) 1865 778315

Asia Pacific
E: cs-journals@wiley.com
T: +65 6511 8000

Japan (for Japanese-speaking support)
E: cs-japan@wiley.com
T: +65 6511 8010 or 005 316 50 480 (toll-free)

Visit our Online Customer Help available in 7 languages at www.wileycustomerhelp .com/ask

Print ISSN: 0003-8504
Online ISSN: 1554-2769

Prices are for six issues and include postage and handling charges. Individual-rate subscriptions must be paid by personal cheque or credit card. Individual-rate subscriptions may not be resold or used as library copies.

All prices are subject to change without notice.

Identification Statement
Periodicals Postage paid at Rahway, NJ 07065. Air freight and mailing in the USA by Mercury Media Processing, 1850 Elizabeth Avenue, Suite C, Rahway, NJ 07065, USA.

USA Postmaster
Please send address changes to *Architectural Design*, c/o Mercury Media Processing, 1634 E. Elizabeth Avenue, Linden, NJ 07036, USA.

Subscribe to ⏃
⏃ is published bimonthly and is available to purchase on both a subscription basis and as individual volumes at the following prices.

Prices
Individual copies:
£24.99 / US$39.95
Individual issues on
⏃ App for iPad:
£9.99 / US$13.99
Mailing fees for print may apply

Annual Subscription Rates
Student: £75 / US$117
print only
Personal: £120 / US$189
print and iPad access
Institutional: £212 / US$398
print or online
Institutional: £244 / US$457
combined print and online
6-issue subscription on
⏃ App for iPad: £44.99 /
US$64.99

⏃ | ARCHITECTURAL DESIGN

March/April	Profile No.
2016	**240**

Front cover: Zaha Hadid Architects, Galaxy Soho, Beijing, China, 2012. © Iwan Baan

Inside front cover: Zaha Hadid Architects, Galaxy Soho, Beijing, China, 2012. © lighting design, LIGHTDESIGN Inc, photo Toshio Kaneko

02/2016

MIX
Paper from
responsible sources
FSC® C015829

EDITORIAL

HELEN CASTLE

Parametricism by its very formulation is controversial. As a term, 'Parametricism' is an inflation of the concept of 'parametric design': the design process that employs variable parameters or algorithms to generate geometries or objects. While parametric design is a matter of methodology and aesthetically agnostic, with the addition of that crucial 'ism' Parametricism takes on all the stylistic and social intentionality of a movement. In an age of pluralism, Parametricism's assertive confidence sets it apart within the architectural community, igniting dissent. (See Mark Burry's description of the architectural 'kerfuffle' it has stirred up on p 32 and Mark Foster Gage's scathing Counterpoint on p 128.) Parametricism is uncompromising and unapologetic in its bid for centre stage. Rather than seeking to accommodate a multitude of simultaneous tendencies or trends, it assuredly aspires to be *the* single universal, global style in a manner that is redolent of Modernism. Like the Modern Movement, it draws its charge and impetus from technological advancement, as described by Guest-editor Patrik Schumacher in the Introduction: 'Parametricism is architecture's answer to contemporary, computationally empowered civilisation, and is the only architectural style that can take full advantage of the computational revolution that now drives all domains of society.' Unlike other architects, who are diffident to the point of being evasive about the formal qualities of their architecture, Schumacher unambiguously advocates Parametricism as a style.

Over the last eight years, Parametricism's ascendancy as a force to be reckoned with in architecture is almost solely due to the output and activities of its main protagonist Patrik Schumacher, Partner at Zaha Hadid Architects (ZHA) and founder/studio master at the Architectural Associations's Design Research Lab (AADRL). Zaha's work, as demonstrated by buildings such as the MAXXI: Italian National Museum of 21st Century Arts in Rome (2009), the Guangzhou Opera House in China (2010), the London Aquatics Centre for the 2012 Olympic Games (2011) and the Heydar Aliyev Centre in Baku (2013), has created some of the most memorable and iconic buildings of our time. Schumacher has been unafraid to take the platform, raise his head above the parapet and unstintingly assert his position and cause debate. This is often in a climate when Zaha's very success has exposed the practice and Parametricism to sniping criticism from other architects and the media. This issue of *D* comes at a time when Schumacher recognises that the tide of fashion is turning and Parametricism is 'externally embattled', losing its sway in leading architectural schools around the world. Through its redefinition of Parametricism, *Parametricism 2.0* embraces this as a moment of questioning through 'self-critical redirection'. This is reflected in the issue by the fact that rather than filling the contents with his own coterie, Schumacher consciously extended the invitation to contribute to renowned thinkers and architects such as John Frazer, Mark Burry and Achim Menges, who might generally be regarded as being comfortably outside Parametricism's fold.

Whatever your response to Parametricism as a formal style, it is apparent that Schumacher's espousal of it as a movement has had a positive impact on contemporary architecture: provoking debate and causing architects with disparate approaches to react and redefine their own positions in riposte. It has also motivated an entire generation of students and emerging architects to skill up and explore advanced computational design techniques. Moreover, as an architecture of the utmost confidence, Parametricism goes out into the world and asserts itself through exciting buildings, enhancing the credence, presence and interest of architectural culture and design among the wider public. *D*

Zaha Hadid Architects (ZHA)

Heydar Aliyev Centre

Baku

Azerbaijan

2012

This national cultural centre comprises a museum, library and concert hall. The design fuses yet also distinguishes the three institutions within its continuous silhouette and surface. The unity-across-differences principle also connects and differentiates the interior spaces.

Patrik Schumacher is partner at Zaha Hadid Architects (ZHA) and co-founder of the Architectural Association Design Research Lab (AADRL) in London. He joined Zaha Hadid in 1988 and has since been co-author of many key projects such as the MAXXI: Museum of XXI Century Arts in Rome (2009), Heydar Aliyev Culture Centre in Baku, Azerbaijan (2012) and Dongdaemun Design Plaza in Seoul (2013). He has been seminal in developing ZHA to become a 450-strong global architecture and design brand.

Schumacher studied philosophy, mathematics and architecture in Bonn, London and Stuttgart, where he received his Diploma in architecture in 1990. In 1999 he completed his PhD at the Institute for Cultural Science, Klagenfurt University. He continues to teach in the AADRL programme, and from 2004 to 2013 was Professor at the Institute for Experimental Architecture at the University of Innsbruck. In 2013 he was appointed as the first John Portman Chair in Architecture at Harvard University's Graduate School of Design (GSD).

In his much-debated *Δ* article 'Parametricism: A New Global Style for Architecture and Urban Design' (2009),[1] Schumacher argued that the global convergence in recent avant-garde architecture justifies the enunciation of a new style – Parametricism – poised to succeed Modernism as a new epochal style for the 21st century. He believes Parametricism is architecture's answer to the momentous technological and socioeconomic transformation of world society brought about by the Information Age. In 2011 he published his treatise *The Autopoiesis of Architecture, Vol.1: A New Framework for Architecture*.[2] The book presents a comprehensive discourse analysis of the discipline, analysing architecture's key distinctions, concepts, values, styles, methods and media. Its central thesis is that the phenomenon of architecture can be most adequately grasped if it is analysed as an autonomous network (autopoietic system) of communications.

The second volume of the treatise – *Vol. 2: A New Agenda for Architecture* – was published in 2012.[3] Here Schumacher proposed a new agenda for contemporary architecture in response to the challenges and opportunities posed by current societal and technological developments. The volume ends with an expanded manifesto for the new epochal style of Parametricism. To be credible, Schumacher argues, a unified style must be backed up and guided by a unified theoretical system that is able to integrate many partial theories: a theory of architecture's societal function, of the discipline's self-demarcation, and of the avant-garde, aesthetic theory, media theory, process theory etc. He asserts that the theory of architectural autopoiesis presents such an integrated theoretical system as the rational reconstruction and systematisation of the discursively evolving discipline, made explicit as unified theory and opened up to criticism and constructive elaboration.

Since the publication of his magnum opus, Schumacher has expanded his research in two related directions, namely the elaboration of a new approach to architectural semiology based on crowd simulation and the investigation of how a legible urban order might emerge on the basis of market processes under the auspices of Parametricism as a global best-practice methodology. *Δ*

Notes
1. Patrik Schumacher, 'Parametricism: A New Global Style for Architecture and Urban Design', in Neil Leach (ed), AD *Digital Cities*, July/August (no 4), 2009.
2. Patrik Schumacher, *The Autopoiesis of Architecture, Vol I: A New Framework for Architecture*, John Wiley & Sons (Chichester), 2011.
3. Patrik Schumacher, *The Autopoiesis of Architecture, Vol II: A New Agenda for Architecture*, John Wiley & Sons (Chichester), 2012.

INTRODUCTION

PATRIK SCHUMACHER

SOM

Terminal 2

Chhatrapati Shivaji
International Airport

Mumbai

India

2014

Gearing Up to Impact the
Global Built Environment

Parametricism 2.0

Since launching 'Parametricism' at the 2008 Venice Architecture Biennale and further consolidating its inception with an article in $\mathcal{D}$ in 2009, the term has gained a wide and established currency within architectural discourse.[1] Its meaning is presupposed here and can be gleaned from the well-written respective Wikipedia entry.[2] But what is the point and meaning of 'Parametricism 2.0'?

Parametricism is evolving internally yet is externally embattled. Its internal evolution needs to accelerate, as well as address and confront its external critics. The aim of this issue of $\mathcal{D}$ is to try to halt and reverse the increasing marginalisation of Parametricism, the evidence for which is apparent in its fading influence within schools of architecture. This turn away from Parametricism is most conspicuous within the former hotbeds of the movement such as the Architectural Association (AA) in London and Columbia University Graduate School of Architecture, Planning and Preservation (GSAPP) in New York. Another indication is the general backlash against 'iconic' architecture in architectural criticism, and the recent proliferation of a frugal Neo-Rationalism. The anti-icon polemic misunderstands that an architecture that is rigorously developed on the basis of radically new, innovative principles becomes conspicuous by default rather than by intention. Both the anti-icon and Neo-Rationalist camps fail to recognise that the new societal complexity calls for urban and architectural complexity.

Within this increasingly hostile environment, $\mathcal{D}$ is not only Parametricism's most important communication platform, but indeed its last high-powered bastion where it maintains a strong (if not dominant) presence. Its many dedicated issues have been Parametricism's organs for theoretical debate and project exposition. Two recent issues of particular pertinence to the new emphasis that Parametricism 2.0 aims to promote within the movement are $\mathcal{D}$ *Computation Works* (2013)[3] and $\mathcal{D}$ *Empathic Space* (2014).[4] The first demonstrates the emphasis on research-based best-practice expertise that can deliver large, important buildings; and the second the new focus on social functionality. Both aspects are crucial for Parametricism to mature from an avant-garde and research-focused movement to the mainstream best practice and global style it deserves to become. If the current backlash against Parametricism succeeds in halting its proliferation and preventing its transformative impact, then the discipline is failing in its raison d'être to innovatively adapt and upgrade the built environment in response to the challenges and opportunities of contemporary civilisation. If retro-rationalism prevails, then the discipline of architecture will once again end up where it was 80 years ago, without any impact on the built environment and with no contribution to society whatsoever.

The embattled state of Parametricism calls for a high-stakes discourse based on: (1) confrontation – a no-holds-barred polemic and criticism of its detractors and supposed alternatives; (2) explication – a positive explanation of its superior rationality that makes explicit its compelling advantages and achievements; and (3) self-criticism: a critical debate within the movement that not only takes to task the superficial epigones that serve to discredit it, but self-critically and constructively debates its most urgent challenges and research agendas. This issue of △ is dedicated to the challenges related to the second and third points above, leaving the equally urgent polemical confrontation to better-suited media.

The Crisis of Parametricism and the Agenda of Parametricism 2.0
In order to reverse the current marginalisation of Parametricism, it is necessary to relaunch it in a self-critical redirection as Parametricism 2.0. Parametricism is architecture's answer to contemporary, computationally empowered civilisation, and is the only architectural style that can take full advantage of the computational revolution that now drives all domains of society. More specifically, it is the only style congenial to recent advances in structural and environmental engineering based on computational analytics and optimisation techniques. All other approaches are incapable of working with the efficiencies of the adaptive structural and tectonic differentiations that issue from new engineering intelligence, forcing its adherents to waste this opportunity and thus to squander resources.

Taking the above performance conditions seriously almost inevitably leads contemporary architects to Parametricism and the geometric transcoding of parameter variations into differentiated geometries. This much pertains to Parametricism's obvious superiority in terms of the technical functionality of the built environment. But what is perhaps less obvious, though by no means less compelling, is its superiority with respect to the advancement of the social functionality of the built environment. Due to its versatile formal and spatio-organisational repertoire, Parametricism is the only contemporary approach that can adequately address the challenges posed to architecture by the new social dynamics of the Information Age. Accordingly, it is already addressing all major urban building tasks, on all scales, including infrastructure projects such as railway stations and airports.

These facts, though, are only rarely appreciated. The functionality of Parametricism – whether technical or social – is usually seen as suspect. Indeed, Parametricist works are not even presumed to aim at performance, and instead are misunderstood as expressions of artistic or technophilic exuberance, or even as esoteric design process fetishism. This is unfortunate, but perhaps excusable, since the functioning of many projects remains indeed suspect, and the discourse of the parametric design movement has not placed enough emphasis on discussion and explication of its practical advantages, especially in the domain of social functionality. While artistic and technological creativity, as well as esoteric internal design process orientation, must still play a part in creating the avant-garde character of Parametricism, this must now recede and give way to a focus on social performance if the movement is to mature, go mainstream and be accepted as a serious contender for global best practice.

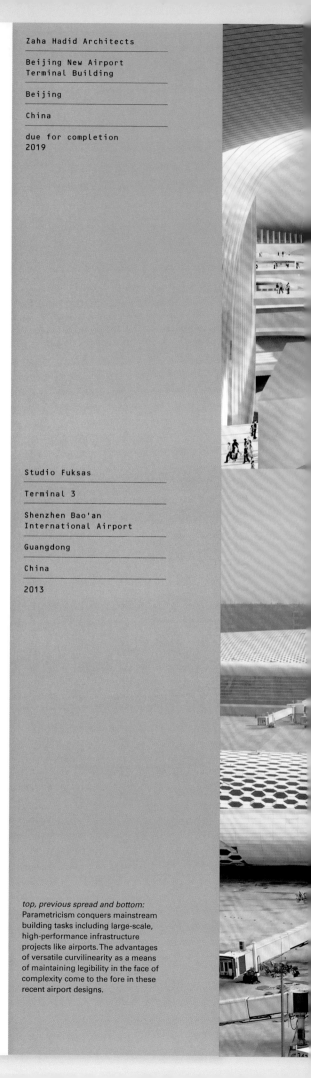

Zaha Hadid Architects

Beijing New Airport
Terminal Building

Beijing

China

due for completion
2019

Studio Fuksas

Terminal 3

Shenzhen Bao'an
International Airport

Guangdong

China

2013

top, previous spread and bottom: Parametricism conquers mainstream building tasks including large-scale, high-performance infrastructure projects like airports. The advantages of versatile curvilinearity as a means of maintaining legibility in the face of complexity come to the fore in these recent airport designs.

Parametricism is architecture's answer
to contemporary, computationally
empowered civilisation ...

However, the 2008 economic crisis and subsequent great recession have slowed down Parametricism's expansion into the mainstream. Moreover, over the last few years of economic stagnation, when investment in spatial and formal complexity was regarded as an indefensible self-indulgence in the face of general austerity, the misleading assessment of the Parametricist movement turned into outright hostility. Parametricism – associated as it is with the profligacy of the boom years – is thus experiencing a crisis of legitimacy. In order to survive and succeed, it must shift its focus away from the foregrounding of formal principles and design processes, and instead place more emphasis on functional principles and societal purposes. Design research should continue, but must become more strategic, applied and performance oriented. This has already started to happen. Parametricism is thus growing up and becoming serious about making an impact in the world.

This issue of Δ gathers together some of the key protagonists of Parametricism and presents important, computationally informed design research in architecture, urbanism and product design, as well as closely related experimental research in structural engineering, fabrication and the application of robotics within the domain of the built environment. As Philippe Block puts it in his contribution to this issue: 'Parametricism needs real structural and engineering innovations to differentiate itself from purely image-driven architecture and to realise the full potential of complex curved geometry' (see pp 68–75). His design research with the Block Research Group (BRG) at ETH Zurich makes the efficiencies of shell structures available for the generation of new and complex freeform shapes, considerably expanding the problem-solving capacity of these super-efficient structural systems. The result, in Block's words, is that 'the terms "expressive" and "structurally efficient" are no longer oxymoronic, but can be synonymous'.

All of the work presented in this Δ shows that the days of adolescent muscle-flexing are over, that the real work has begun, in terms of serious research and realised projects that excel in technical as well as social functionality, and that Parametricism can now take on relevant, high-performance projects.

The issue begins with reflections on the historical precursors and recent history of Parametricism as a backdrop for its current achievements and a guide map for its future trajectory. John Frazer's 'Parametric Computation: History and Future' (pp 18–23) describes the history of computation within architecture/design, emphasising the far-sighted vision of the pioneers of the 1960s and 1970s that was lost with the commercial uptake of computer-aided design (CAD) as a mechanical drafting tool in the 1980s, and then rediscovered in the generative systems of the late 1990s. Parametricism is now espousing the values that inspired and motivated these pioneers.

Mario Carpo's short history of Parametricism – 'Parametric Notations: The Birth of the Non-Standard' (pp 24–9) – then makes the point that it was the exuberant formalists such as Frank Gehry, Peter Eisenman, Zaha Hadid and Wolf Prix who were the first to make computation impactful within architecture in the early 1990s, while the more serious

The organisation of the project includes three permanent museums, a library, several large exhibition halls and workshop spaces. It provides a national hub for popular education as well as elite communication for the creative arts, for example as host to Seoul Fashion Week. The building sponsors an urban park and gives shape and orientation to a complex inner-city site, providing intuitive access from multiple levels and directions.

cybernetic experiments of the 1960s and 1970s – and the pioneers Frazer celebrates – in Carpo's words 'did not change architecture at all'. Carpo emphasises that architects have been at the forefront of technological innovation and expressed the logic and opportunities of digital tools better than most other professions.

However, a generalisable real-world impact can only be expected when the playfully discovered opportunities are systematically applied by yet another cast of characters: the protagonists/authors of this issue. The current protagonists of Parametricism have been deeply impressed and influenced by the profoundly innovative work of Antoni Gaudí and Frei Otto, who must be recognised as its predigital precursors. According to Mark Burry, the

parametric work of Gaudí and Otto is countering any claim that Parametricism is merely a contemporary digital condition (see his article on pp 30–35). (This point is further supported by Frazer's reminder about Luigi Moretti's 'Architettura Parametrica', as well as by Carpo's suggestion that the procedural geometrical rules of Gothic building can be understood as parametric algorithms.) Recognition of these precursors is coherent with my own insistence on the independence and distinction of Parametricism as a paradigm, methodology and style from the use of digital tools per se. However, computational empowerment and coding has become increasingly important for the current and future ambitions of Parametricism 2.0.

Zaha Hadid Architects

3D-printed chair prototype

2014

above and below: ZHACODE is exploiting the morphological intricacy made possible by 3D printing to take full advantage of form-finding and structural optimisation techniques such as shell formation via particle spring mesh relaxation and evolutionary topology optimisation for rib- and perforation patterns.

Minimaforms

Emotive City

2015

opposite: Emotive City is a speculative model for the contemporary city where the fabric of clustered living environments is conceived to assemble and reassemble on the basis of a collective intelligence that is local and relational.

Towards a Constructive Division of Labour Within Parametricism 2.0

The relative maturity of Parametricism is evident in the emerging division of labour among various parallel research and design trajectories. One of the most future-oriented strands of design research based on advanced computing and machine intelligence is pushed forward at the Architectural Association Design Research Lab (AADRL) and documented here in the contributions of Shajay Bhooshan, Theodore Spyropoulos and Robert Stuart-Smith.

Bhooshan's 'Upgrading Computational Design' (pp 44–53) depicts the dense network of cumulative, interdisciplinary research and design collaborations involving academic institutions as well as professional firms and their specialist groups. Such research across disciplines and authors/designers presupposes the well-established paradigm of Parametricism as the shared basis of all these combined and complementary efforts, where it delivers a robust platform for advanced professional work and also sets the scene and gives a credible grounding for radically future-oriented projects. And it is in this context that the computationally advanced, speculative work at the AADRL where Bhooshan teaches, and at Zaha Hadid Architects (ZHA) where he leads the computational design group ZHACODE, must be viewed.

In 'Behavioural Complexity: Constructing Frameworks for Human–Machine Ecologies' (pp 36–43), Spyropoulos (at the AADRL and with his practice Minimaforms) conceives architecture as an ecology of interacting agents and investigates the behavioural agency of autonomous self-aware and self-assembled systems that use responsiveness and machine learning to facilitate continuous spatial transformation. Here, architecture senses, learns and stimulates. Stuart-Smith's 'Behavioural Production: Autonomous Swarm-Constructed Architecture' (pp 54–9) presents robotic construction processes that are orchestrated through real-time autonomous and semi-autonomous behavioural rules that govern event-driven robotic building actions. This research envisages that design and production processes are fused within a single algorithm, and so recasts construction as a creative and qualitative design act in its own right. The experiments realised with drones demonstrate that the technologies required for this ambitious programme are in place.

Between university-based academic and professional work exists another channel (and funding mechanism) for ambitious design research: the art world. For Marc Fornes (working under the banner of THEVERYMANY), as indeed for most of the protagonists presented in this issue, the art world serves as a way station along the route from avant-garde speculation to mainstream realisation. (This is indeed a large part of the art world's societal function.) In his contribution 'The Art of the Prototypical' (pp 60–67), Fornes demonstrates Parametricism's capacity to manage a new, previously unimaginable level of geometric variation and complexity.

This impressive ability is harnessed for intricate spatial, structural and aesthetic effects with a surprising economy of means. All morphologies result from explicit and encoded protocols involving large numbers of very small, relatively

simple, similar but variable (mostly laser-cut) parts. Fornes's computational techniques allow him to incorporate structural optimisation as well as fabrication constraints. Although the result is the sum of deterministic steps, and the author wrote every line of code, it is impossible for him to anticipate the outcome exactly due to the number of lines, steps and 'if-then' statements. Objective determinacy is thus coupled with subjective indeterminacy that spurns explorative series working. Fornes calls this 'generative assembly' and 'protocol form-finding'. It is only a matter of time before this work migrates from art back to architecture, a process that is already well under way.

The work of Achim Menges at the Institute for Computational Design (ICD) at the University of Stuttgart charts a very similar trajectory, from experimental installations and pavilions into architecture proper, with a similar focus on structural optimisations and fabrication logics. His article 'Computational Material Culture' (pp 76–83) demonstrates that material is no longer a passive receptor of predetermined form, but rather an active driver of architectural design. According to Menges, 'computation is not limited to processes that operate only in the digital domain. Instead, it has been recognised that material processes also obtain a computational capacity – the ability to physically compute form'. His contribution presents design research on the integration of these two modes of computation: the computational convergence of the processes of form generation and materialisation.

The computational grasp of parameter-dependent processes of emergence and transformation is also a winning proposition in the field of urban planning and design. In their contribution 'Relational Urban Models: Parameters, Values and Tacit Forms of Algorithms' (pp 84–91), Enriqueta Llabres and Eduardo Rico present an urban design methodology based on the use of Relational Urban Models (RUMs). These Web-based participatory models involve the simultaneous visualisation of design variables, 3D massing and landform dynamics that allows for discussion of how urban form is influenced by, and influences, various infrastructural, economic and environmental parameters. The models might be crafted to extract knowledge about preferences and simulate the results for setting the incentive parameters of the various stakeholders involved. Their longer-term potential is in enhancing the quality and precision of the debates and negotiations that shape urban policies and, ultimately, our cities.

Parametricism, with its core value of adaptivity, includes adaptation to regional specificities. This implies that its global reach does not – as International Modernism did – spell global homogenisation. In fact, Parametricism offers the promise of a re-specification of regional identities.

In his article 'Parametric Regionalism' (pp 92–9), Philip Yuan of Archi-Union Architects explains that 'Regionalism … addresses not only local craftsmanship, but also local climate, site information, local culture and behaviour'. He demonstrates this approach with his practice's work in China, creatively synthesising local materials and craft traditions with advanced computational design techniques to deliver technological and social innovations without violating cultural expectations.

As a matter of principle, and just as was the case with Modernism, the scope of Parametricism as an epochal style encompasses all the design disciplines, including industrial product design. However, a principle takes on reality only via historical actors. These are still sparse when it comes to realising Parametricism's claim to universal and exclusive competency with respect to the world of artefacts. All the more important, therefore, are the partisan commitment to and exemplary spearheading efforts of Ross Lovegrove's genius against the grain of the stubborn conservatism of the industrial design sector. In his contribution 'Super-Natural: Parametricism in Product Design' (pp 100–107), Lovegrove explains how his diverse biomorphic designs, encompassing categories like vehicle design, furniture and fashion, are unified by being governed by 'genesis principles that combine structure, material and minimal mass' aiming for an 'Organic Essentialism' that is inspired by 'nature's economic sincerity'. His compelling products are bound to convince the world of Parametricism's superiority more than any theoretical treatise ever can.

Only Parametricism can adequately organise and articulate contemporary social assemblages at the level of complexity called for today.

MARC FORNES/THEVERYMANY

nonLin/Lin

FRAC Centre

Orléans

France

2011

This ultra-light 'generative assembly' structure is based on a deterministic, recursive rule that takes account of both structural and fabrication constraints.

Institute for Computational Design (Achim Menges) and Institute of Building Structures and Structural Design (Jan Knippers)

ICD/ITKE Research Pavilion 2012

University of Stuttgart

2012

The pavilion heralds the emergence of a novel 'computational material culture' as described in Achim Menges's contribution to the issue (see pp 76–83). It explores the architectural and structural potentials offered by integral computational design and fabrication processes that utilise the self-forming capacity of glass and carbon fibres.

Notes
1. Patrik Schumacher, 'Parametricism as Style – Parametricist Manifesto', presented and discussed at the Dark Side Club, 11th Architecture Biennale, Venice, 2008: www.patrikschumacher. com/Texts/Parametricism%20as%20 Style.htmPatrik; and Patrik Schumacher, 'Parametricism: A New Global Style for Architecture and Urban Design', in Neil Leach (ed), *D Digital Cities*, July/ August (no 4), 2009, pp 14–23.
2. https://en.wikipedia.org/wiki/ Parametricism.
3. Brady Peters and Xavier de Kestelier (eds), *D Computation Works: The Building of Algorithmic Thought*, March/April (no 2), 2013.
4. Christian Derix and Åsmund Izaki (eds), *D Empathic Space: The Computation of Human-Centric Architecture*, September/October (no 5), 2014.
5. Patrik Schumacher, 'Tectonic Articulation: Making Engineering Logics Speak', in Mark Garcia (ed), *D Future Details of Architecture*, July/ August (no 4), 2014, pp 44–51.
6. Patrik Schumacher, *The Autopoiesis of Architecture, Vol II: A New Agenda for Architecture*, John Wiley & Sons (Chichester), 2012.

My own two contributions in the issue – 'Advancing Social Functionality Via Agent-Based Parametric Semiology' (pp 108–13) and 'Hegemonic Parametricism Delivers Market-Based Urban Order' (pp 114–23) – take Parametricism's potential for unmatched technological superiority for granted to focus on and demonstrate its performance with respect to social functionality. The concept of 'social functionality' is meant to pinpoint the purpose and thus the primary criterion of design projects in terms of the requirements of today's society (as mediated via clients). It refers to the social processes that should be congenially accommodated and organised by architecture's spatial creations.

Architecture's communicative capacity is crucial here, and as such should be regarded as its core competency. The elaboration of spatial complexes as systems-of-signification is key to upgrading this. The meaning of the designed architectural code can be revealed via agent-based crowd modelling, where the modulation of the agent's behavioural rules is made dependent on the configurational and morphological features of the environment designed in accordance with a semiological code, and where programmed agents respond to environmental clues. Thus these new tools allow for the re-foundation of architectural semiology as agent-based parametric semiology.

But how does the work of Burry, Bhooshan, Spyropoulos, Stuart-Smith, Fornes, Menges, Yuan and Lovegrove relate to this semiological project? As I have argued in a previous issue of D,[5] the outcomes of these protagonists' design research efforts in the domain of technical functionality furnish the crucial, congenial repertoire for semiological articulation within the context of a much more differentiated contemporary society. The substantive, material motivation of morphological differentiations gives a special credibility to the semiological code that we cannot expect from an unmotivated, wholly arbitrary symbolic language. Structure does not lie, and nor do the other technical performance constraints that drive parametric morphogenesis.

Identifiable, information-rich morphologies are inherent in Parametricism's methodology. In my second contribution to this issue of D, I pose the question: How can the vital desire for urban order, identity and legibility be reconciled with the seemingly uncontrollable, market-driven processes of contemporary urbanisation? Beginning in the 1970s, the historical urban results so far are negative: disorder abounds and urban identities are being more and more eroded. How can the ambitions of Parametric urbanism – as espoused by myself and by protagonists such as Enriqueta Llabres and Eduardo Rico – find a foothold in reality in a context of receding planning authority? The answer: Freedom and order beyond the bounds of planning can emerge via the discursive convergence of the design disciplines towards a new epochal style: Parametricism.

To continuously update and upgrade its societal relevance and its ability to self-steer its practice, Parametricism must engage with contemporary social theory. Manuel DeLanda's 'Parametrising the Social' (pp 124–7) is therefore a contemporary approach to the study of society and its social processes that is congenial to the theoretical underpinnings and methodology of Parametricism. Here, DeLanda posits that between the micro-scale of individuals and the macro-scale of society as a whole there operates an important meso-scale of intermediately sized social entities: communities, organisations, cities and urban regions. These are theorised as decomposable yet irreducible assemblages with emergent properties on multiple, recursive levels of emergence. DeLanda is thus steering clear of both holism and reductionism. Assemblages are 'always concretely embodied and spatially situated'; that is, they usually include boundaries, buildings and other physico-spatial infrastructures.

Significantly, DeLanda proposes two dimensions within which social assemblages are parametrised: the degree of territorialisation or deterritorialisation, and that of coding or decoding. Both dimensions involve architecture. In my theory of architectural autopoiesis,[6] these dimensions feature under the labels of organisation and (semiological) articulation respectively. Only Parametricism can adequately organise and articulate contemporary social assemblages at the level of complexity called for today. D

John Frazer

Parametric Computation

History and Future

John Frazer is a pioneer and leader in the field of generative design and evolutionary computation. In the 1970s he developed the world's first microcomputer-based design systems and invented tangible interfaces. Professor at the European Graduate School, he is the author of the seminal book *An Evolutionary Architecture* (1995). Here he traces the history of parametric architecture and discusses how, in its second state, redefined as Parametricism 2.0, Parametricism opens up the possibilities to become more than a matter of generational technique, scripting variational geometry, and a means to addressing wider social and environmental purpose.

Varying parameters, which respond to the iterations of an algorithm, are the basis of computation. This article briefly outlines the history of parametric architecture and shows how 'Parametricism 2.0' now proposes to return to addressing the environmental and social issues for which these powerful generative and evolutionary techniques were originally developed.

When in the mid-20th century computing absorbed the language of variables and parameters from mathematics, it adopted the terminology for programmable algorithms and procedures. The first documented computer programs were written by Ada Lovelace in 1843 for Charles Babbage's proposed analytical engine and were based on his algorithms. These algorithms were based on varying parameters in a series of loops that Ada called 'backing' but were in fact the first uses of loops and conditional jumps.[1] The pioneers of digital design, such as Ivan Sutherland with his 1963 Sketchpad system, developed an essentially parametric system for architectural design.[2] Computer-aided design went on in the 1970s to fully assimilate parametrics, which is thus described now by Mark Burry as the 'sine qua non' of design computation.[3]

Architettura Parametrica

When it came to parametric architecture, the concept and use of the term again predated the feasibility of using actual computational processes, and appears to have originated from the Italian architect Luigi Moretti in the 1940s when he coined the term *'Architettura Parametrica'*.[4] Moretti researched the relationship between architectural design and parametric equations under the banner of 'Architettura Parametrica' between 1940 and 1942,[5] initially without the benefits of computers. However, by 1960, with the aid of a 610 IBM computer, he was able to exhibit models of parametrically designed stadia – *Progetti di strutture per lo sport e lo spettacolo* – at the XII Triennale di Milano.

The earlier work of Antoni Gaudí is also essentially parametric. However, we know this not from his own writings, but due to the painstaking and insightful post-analysis work by Mark Burry that is currently assisting the reconstruction of the intended forms of the Spanish architect's uncompleted Sagrada Família Basilica in Barcelona (see Burry's article on pp 30–35 of this issue). The parametric computation here should perhaps then be credited to Burry rather than to Gaudí. Though there are even earlier examples of parametrically described three-dimensional forms, it would seem that Moretti was probably the first to create three-dimensional architectural form using a complex set of parametric relationships resolved by digital computation.[6]

Luigi Moretti

Model of parametrically designed sports stadium

XII Triennale di Milano

1960

Drawing after Luigi Moretti by CHK Design

Moretti worked on a parametric design process from 1940 onwards and appears to have originated the concept of parametric design as *'Architettura Parametrica'*, which he published before the development of computers. This series of *'Progetti di strutture per lo sport e lo spettacolo'* was realised later when he had access to the necessary computational power and was exhibited at the XII Triennale di Milano in 1960.

Parametric Design Now

Parametric design as now understood is not fundamentally different from the way Moretti described it in the 1940s, but the terminology has changed. A usefully loose definition by Wassim Jabi reads: 'Parametric Design: A process based on algorithmic thinking that enables the expression of parameters and rules that, together, define, encode and clarify the relationship between design intent and design response.'[7]

The parametric design process is dependent on a parametric model, and Patrick Janssen differentiates several kinds of parametric modelling techniques – object modelling, associative, dataflow and procedural – that mainly vary in their ability to support iteration.[8] He defines a parametric model as:

> an algorithm that generates models consisting of geometry and attributes (e.g. material definitions). This algorithm uses functions and variables, including both dependent and independent variables. Some of the

independent variables can be given a more prominent status, as the interface to the parametric model – these are referred to as the parameters of the model.[9]

The advantage of this definition is that it leads to an understanding of how different parametric systems can have very different styles, and indeed can be used to define those styles. Consider a classical column that has parameters that define the proportional relationships between the elements of, say, the base, capital and entablature, and the specific dimensions of an instance of the column for a particular application that is controlled by a variable, such as column height. All other dimensions, such as the diameter, are dependent variables and produced automatically from the proportioning rules controlled by the parameters.[10]

Just as changing the parameters of the proportioning rules changes the style of a classical column from Doric to Ionic, so too does the style of, say, a building by Zaha Hadid Architects depend on the parameters controlling the

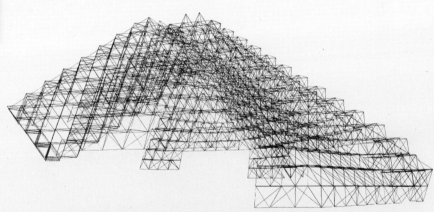

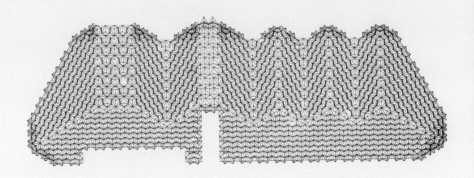

John Frazer

Parametric design program for the Reptile Structural System

Architectural Association (AA) and the University of Cambridge

1969

right (both): Frazer's concept-seeding technique used to develop complex enclosure structures parametrically from a minimal seed of structural units.

above: The parametric design program on-screen in the University of Cambridge Mathematical Laboratory in 1969. A parametrically controlled seed being interactively developed on-screen for the first time, in accordance with Frazer's rules.

relationships between the geometrical elements and the use of iterative generative procedures to control the variables of a specific instantiation. The parameters selected by an architect to define the style and its aesthetics are a very small subset of possible parameters that could be varied, and that selection is what gives that architectural style a particular appearance, perhaps a currently fashionable Baroque curvilinearity. But the selection and definition of a different set of parameters can just as easily lead to a minimalist rectilinear aesthetic, for example. In fact, the use of parametrics as such does not necessarily lead to any style at all, and is just an efficient way of flexibly describing geometry, which led Burry to remark in 2011 that non-parametric design was now inconceivable.[11]

In due course Patrik Schumacher coined the term 'Parametricism' to indicate a stylistic intentionality,[12] and then, more recently, 'Parametricism 2.0' to emphasise a second phase focused on addressing real-world social and environmental problems, which is what the originators of parametrics intended from the outset.

Parametricism

In describing, defining and positioning Parametricism, Schumacher's two volumes on *The Autopoiesis of Architecture*[13] reveal a significant ambivalence and duality of meaning. He describes it both as a style in the visual sense, or 'physiognomy' in his terminology, and also as a process-driven architecture in terms of a method. Firstly he establishes the goal as massively ambitious and all-embracing:

> Parametricism is the great new style after Modernism.[14]

> It is now gearing up to go mainstream to finally succeed Modernism in changing the physiognomy of the global built environment.[15]

He goes on to identify the new style by its visual characteristics:

> There is a strong, global convergence in recent avant-garde architecture that justifies the enunciation of

... the use of parametrics as such does not necessarily lead to any style at all, and is just an efficient way of flexibly describing geometry

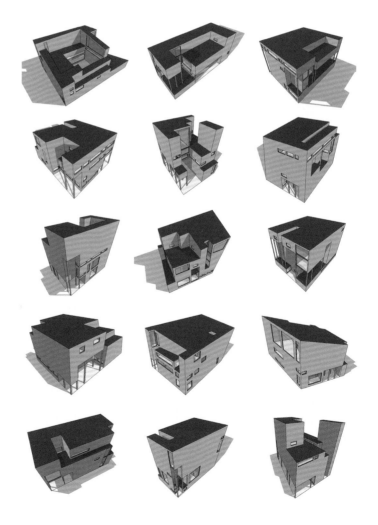

Patrick Janssen and John Frazer

A generative evolutionary design method

Hong Kong Polytechnic University

2004

A set of generative rules defines a parametric space that includes a wide variety of feasible designs, but at the same time excludes all non-feasible ones.

a new style: Parametricism. Its most conspicuous outward characteristic is a complex and dynamic curvilinearity accentuated by a swarm-like proliferation of continuously differentiated components.[16]

He then refers to the new methods:

Beyond such obvious surface features one can identify a series of new concepts and methods that are so different from the repertoire of both traditional and modern architecture that one is justified in speaking of the emergence of a new paradigm within architecture. New design tools play a crucial part in making this possible, establishing a whole new design process and methodology. … Parametricism is thus dependent on the adoption of sophisticated computational techniques. However as a style rather than as a mere panoply of new techniques, Parametricism is characterised by its new distinctive values and sensibilities that started to emerge even before the computational methods were ready to hand.[17]

And finally he writes: 'An architectural style is a coherent and comprehensive (research) programme, complete with both a functional and a formal heuristic.'[18]

Schumacher's *Autopoiesis* books thus clearly embrace process and research as essential elements of a style in the visual sense of the word (although that meaning is strongly embraced too).

Adding Power to Parametrics

Parametric functions in software allow for variable geometries, but do not in themselves drive the generation of form. To build a morphogenetic generative system, further elements are required, which though frequently thought of as associated with parametrics, are not essentially part of it nor indeed usually encoded within the parametric graphics system. These are a generative engine, selection procedure, learning algorithm and a complete design system from inception to development, optimisation and resolution. Such a complete and mature system is typified by my 'Evolutionary Digital Design Method' and described in *An Evolutionary Architecture* (1995).[19]

But we have much further to go yet. Architecture does not address trivial problems, so a computer program of sufficient complexity to play an active role in building design needs to learn skills far beyond the knowledge and experience of the programmer. We are currently still using algorithmic procedures despite the fact that architectural design is obviously not an algorithmic process. This does not mean that algorithms are not useful, just that scripting is simply not enough to address anything more than variational geometry: 'If all we have achieved is to replace drawing with typing then we have achieved nothing!'.[20] However, I believe scripting is now finished and that entirely new environments and media for design will soon be available that employ far more powerful techniques than have yet been tried outside of the research lab.[21]

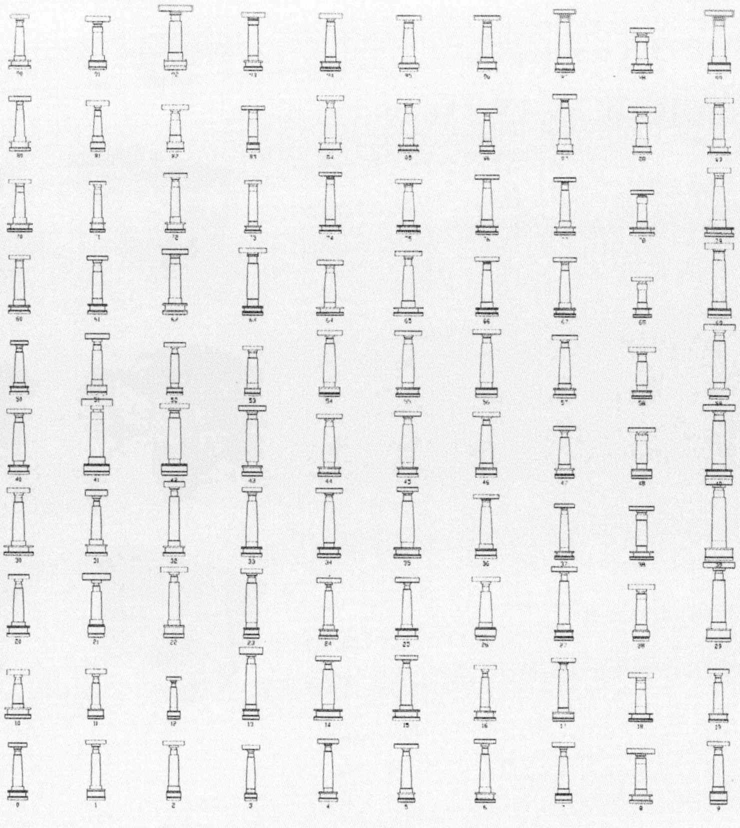

John Frazer and Peter Graham

Evolving a Tuscan column using the parametric rules of James Gibbs (1732) and genetic algorithms

Ulster University

Belfast

1990

A population of 100 columns at generation 6 in the evolution of the proportions of the column controlled by the rules of Gibbs with a genetic algorithm controlling the variations.

Parametricism Redefined

Parametricism is demonstrably moving to redefine itself as a process – a rapidly developing one that embraces new technologies and social and environmental purpose. Earlier works with a particular aesthetic will come to be understood as explorations and feasibility studies under the narrower definition of style, to achieve clarity of differentiation from other styles and approaches, and to test whether the computer techniques of the time were workable and contractors could cope with the new demands of working purely from a digital model. Thus Parametricism (1.0) will soon be re-described as the testing phase, and Parametricism 2.0 will move on to apply powerful computational techniques to real and pressing social and environmental problems.

Or in Moretti's words:

> In this way what I have long solicited and call 'parametric architecture' will be born. Its ineluctable geometric character, its rigorous concatenation of forms, the absolute freedom of fantasy that will spring up in places where equations cannot fix their own roots, will give it a crystalline splendour.[22]

Parametric architecture 'opens for future architecture a whole world of new and revolutionary forms; a new human behaviour of the highest dignity.'[23] △

Notes

1. Michelle Lane, 'Recovering Ada: Finding Our Way Home Through Sensuous Correspondence', unpublished Master's thesis, European Graduate School, 2015. See also Luigi Federico Menabrea, *Sketch of the Analytical Engine invented by Charles Babbage*, translated and appended with additional notes by Augusta Ada, Countess of Lovelace. Richard & John Taylor (London), 1843.
2. Robert Woodbury, *Elements of Parametric Design*, Routledge (London and New York), 2010.
3. Mark Burry, *Scripting Cultures*, John Wiley & Sons (Chichester), 2011, p 18.
4. Federico Bucci and Marco Mulazzani, *Luigi Moretti: Works and Writings*, Princeton Architectural Press (New York), 2002.
5. Luigi Moretti, 'Struttura come forma', *Spazio*, 3 (6), December 1951–April 1952.
6. Daniel Davis, 'A History of Parametric', 6 August 2013: www.danieldavis.com/a-history-of-parametric/.
7. Wassim Jabi, *Parametric Design for Architecture*, Laurence King (London), 2013, p 201.
8. Patrick Janssen and Rudi Stouffs, 'Types of Parametric Modelling', *Proceedings of the 20th International Conference of the Association for Computer-Aided Architectural Design Research in Asia (CAADRIA)*, Daegu, South Korea, 2015, pp 157–66.
9. Patrick Janssen, personal communication to the author, 9 July 2015.
10. Peter Graham, 'The Application of Rule-based Techniques in Computer Aided Design', doctorate thesis supervised by John Frazer, University of Ulster, 1996.
11. Mark Burry, *op cit*, p 18.
12. Patrik Schumacher, 'Parametricism as Style – Parametricist Manifesto', presented and discussed at the Dark Side Club, 11th Architecture Biennale, Venice, 2008: www.patrikschumacher.com/Texts/Parametricism%20as%20Style.htm.
13. Patrik Schumacher, *The Autopoiesis of Architecture, Vol I: A New Framework for Architecture* and *Vol II: A New Agenda for Architecture*, John Wiley & Sons (Chichester), 2011 and 2012.
14. *Ibid*, Vol II, p 617.
15. *Ibid*, Vol II, p 619.
16. *Ibid*, Vol II, p 617.
17. *Ibid*, Vol II, p 617.
18. *Ibid*, Vol II, p 244.
19. John Frazer, 'Creative Design and the Generative Evolutionary Paradigm', in Peter J Bentley and David W Corne, *Creative Evolutionary Systems*, Morgan Kaufmann (San Francisco, CA), 2002, pp 253–74, and John Frazer, *An Evolutionary Architecture*, Architectural Association (London), 1995.
20. John Frazer, as quoted in Mark Burry, *op cit*, p 64.
21. For example the work of the John and Julia Frazer Foundation is developing new environments and media for architectural creativity.
22. Moretti, *op cit*.
23. Luigi Moretti, 'Ricerca matematica in architettura e urbabanisica', *Moebius: unità della cultura: architettura, urbanistica, arte*, IV, 1, 1971, pp 30–53.

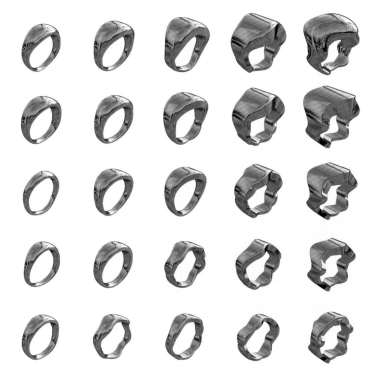

Thomas Fischer and Christiane Herr

Parametric jewellery design and fabrication system

proposed demonstration for a future exhibition

2015

Computer renderings of ring shapes generated using the parametric jewellery design and fabrication system. Eighteen physical sliders in the exhibition would control the parameters to produce a wide variety of shapes while maintaining control of the design aesthetic.

Mario Carpo

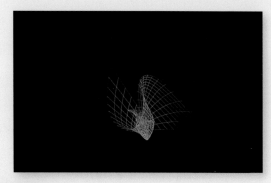

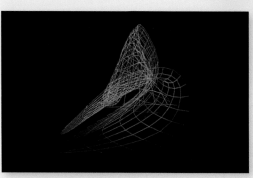

PARAMETRIC
NOTATIONS

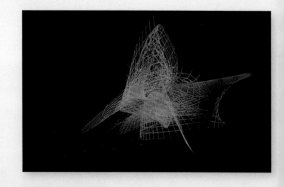

Manit Rastogi, Evolving virtual
environment, Architectural
Association (AA) Diploma Unit 11,
London, 1994

A prototype sequence testing the development,
evolution and mapping of an experiment in the
collaborative evolution of a virtual environment
by global participation on the Internet.

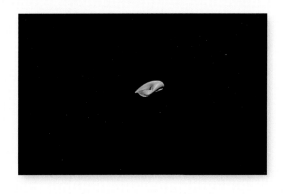

THE BIRTH
OF THE
NON-STANDARD

The use of scripted parameters that define objects in architecture is generally regarded as a recent phenomenon, associated with digital design. **Mario Carpo**, Reyner Banham Professor of Architectural Theory and History at the Bartlett School of Architecture, University College London (UCL), describes how parametric notations are part of an enduring architectural lineage that has its roots in the theses of classical antiquity and the Middle Ages, previous to printing, when the only means of disseminating the proportions and combining of elements was to describe them, writing them out by hand without the aid of illustration.

John Frazer, Julia Frazer, Manit Rastogi,
Patrick Janssen and Peter Graham,
An experiment in global cooperation to evolve
a virtual environment on the Internet,
Architectural Association (AA) Diploma Unit 11,
London, 1994

John Frazer's and Manit Rastogi's work at the AA in London in the early 1990s is an example of the transition from the procedural interests of early cybernetics to the digital formalism of the early 1990s.

Digital Parametricism, as we know it today, was born on page 26 of the first edition of Gilles Deleuze's book *The Fold*, published in French in 1988.[1] In that chapter Deleuze famously tried to come to terms with the modernity of Leibniz's differential calculus – which, in retrospect, was an odd thing to do for a founding father of postmodern philosophy. The way it is still taught in school, calculus notates mathematical functions using variables (X,Y...) and parameters (a, b, c ...). With parameters written in instead of numbers, the script of a function represents a generic family of curves; when parameters are replaced by numbers, the script notates one specific function. Thus, the equation $y = ax^2 + bx + c$ represents all parabolas, and the equation $y = 2x^2 + 3x + 4$ (where the parameters a, b and c are replaced by the numbers 2, 3, 4 respectively) notates one parabola in particular.

Deleuze was intrigued by the generality of the parametric notation, and he suggested that this new kind of general script, which defines a whole set of objects but none in particular, should be called an 'objectile' (whereby he meant: a generic object). Deleuze then went on to say that a gifted student of his, Bernard Cache, had pointed out that this mode of parametric notation is best suited to the logic of computer-based design and fabrication, and best defines the new non-standard technical object of the digital age.[2]

That was in 1988. The rest is history: since the early 1990s, digital Parametricism has changed world architecture. The term was forcefully reinstated in architectural discourse by Patrik Schumacher, and thanks in particular to the outreach and popularity of his recent writings, Parametricism has come to be seen as almost synonymous with digitally intelligent architecture: a new style that exploits and extols, interprets and gives visible form to the technical logic of the new digital tools for design and fabrication.[3]

At the same time, and well beyond the confines of architecture and design, the logic of digital Parametricism has changed, or is poised to change, the way we produce and consume almost everything – and, together with the technical basis of our civilisation, it has already changed the world in which we live. The design professions

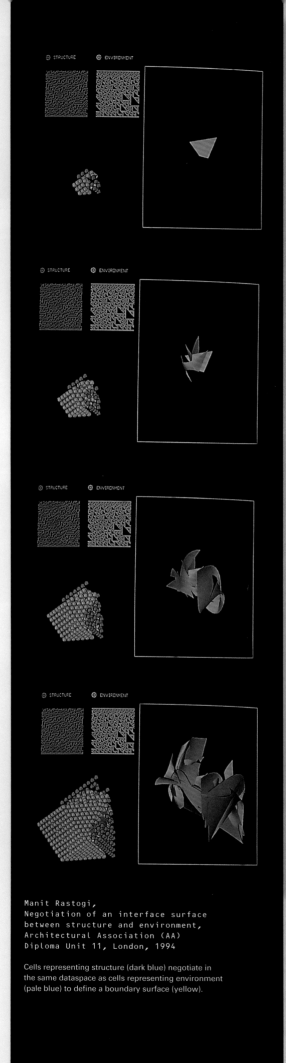

Manit Rastogi,
Negotiation of an interface surface
between structure and environment,
Architectural Association (AA)
Diploma Unit 11, London, 1994

Cells representing structure (dark blue) negotiate in the same dataspace as cells representing environment (pale blue) to define a boundary surface (yellow).

have some reasons to celebrate: for better or worse, digital Parametricism was discovered, nurtured, developed and brought to fame by architects and designers, and adopted by the design professions well before all others. To this day, schools of architecture are at the avant-garde of digital innovation, and the new frontiers of computation are being tested by a new generation of designers and digital makers – not by scientists, economists, lawyers or engineers. Possibly for the first time ever, the design professions – always technological laggards – have been the initiators and the protagonists of a major technological breakthrough. With success, however, often comes a quest for the legitimacy of historical precedent. Sure enough, digital Parametricism was not born out of thin air; witness the very same Deleuzian connection to modern mathematics, the logic (if not the technique) of digital Parametricism is deeply rooted in history, and it descends from an illustrious ancestry.

CYBERNETICS DID NOT BEGET PARAMETRICISM

Electronic computers have been around since the mid-20th century, and recent studies have emphasised the continuity between electronic art in the 1960s and 1970s and the rise of digitally intelligent architecture in the early 1990s. Indeed, some of the protagonists of the early age of cybernetics also went on to participate directly in the digital turn of the 1990s and beyond – think, for example, of the singular career of John Frazer (see his article on pp 18–23 of this issue); the architectural interests and collaborations of Gordon Pask are also well documented.[4]

For all that, no cybernetic architecture ever came to light. Some cyberneticists of the 1960s and 1970s may have been more prescient than others, but when the digital turn in architecture came for good – in the early 1990s – it happened in ways that no one had anticipated. Graphic user interfaces and spline modellers then favoured an easier, more intuitive approach to computer-aided design, and the new digital tools were eagerly adopted by Deconstructivist and formalist designers (old and young alike) who needed them

to design and build complex geometries and non-geometrical objects. The revolution of digital Parametricism in architecture in the 1990s was all about the making of architectural form.

That may seem a truism, but it is nonetheless the main divide between the digital turn that changed architecture in the 1990s and the cybernetic experiments of the 1960s and 1970s, which did not change architecture at all. The spirit of cybernetics may have pervaded the technological exuberance of the early British high-tech, but when Peter Eisenman, Zaha Hadid, Frank Gehry or Wolf Prix went digital, they did not look for inspiration to Archigram or to the Centre Pompidou. In fact, quite the opposite.

PARAMETRICISM AND VARIABILITY IN HISTORY

Parametricism in architecture has a much longer history than that, and the true precedent to today's computational variability must be found in the architectural theory of pre-mechanical civilisations, which in the West include classical antiquity as well as the Middle Ages. For example, both Vitruvius (1st century BC) and

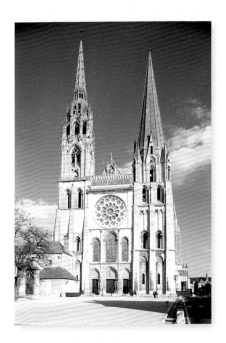

Chartres Cathedral, France, 1194–c 1230

The west facade of Chartres Cathedral (French Gothic architecture, for the most part built in the early 13th century). Regardless of the vicissitudes of its realisation (which took almost four centuries), the west end epitomises a technical culture where the reproduction of identical copies was irrelevant as well as unattainable.

Leon Battista Alberti (1404–72) wrote manuscript treatises meant to be hand-copied without any images or illustrations. So, when explaining how to build a column (Doric, Ionic and so on), they could spell out verbal rules on the proportions and stacking of parts, but could not offer any visual example of what these parts should actually look like – as they had no images to refer to.

Some of Vitruvius's rules, in particular, were astoundingly sophisticated, often in the format of a sequence of if-then clauses that was similar to what today we would call a 'procedural algorithm' (for example: if the height of a column is comprised between a and b, the modular proportions of the architrave should be X; if comprised between b and c, the modular proportions of the architrave should be Y, etc).[5] Furthermore, as the end product could not be shown, verbal instructions could only generate a vast swath of different forms – all different yet all similar, as they all shared a common script. Thus in Vitruvius's and Alberti's treatises the Corinthian capital, for example, is not an object, but a class of objects, mathematically defined by generative rules – in today's terms, an objectile (albeit one defined by discrete, not by continuous variations).

Similar formulaic, and mostly oral geometrical rules presided over medieval building. The few still extant described the making of Gothic spires or pinnacles, but the process was the same for all parts of any major building, and, like those of Vitruvius and Alberti, medieval rules explained how to make an object step by step, but did not (and could not) determine the shape of each individual piece. Consequently, architectural parts with the same function and position in Gothic buildings (say, all ribs in the same pillar, all capitals at the same level in the nave of a cathedral, or all traceries in the same row of windows) are often similar, but seldom identical to one another: they all belong to the same class (or genus), but each one is individually different, or, in a sense, special (from species, as opposed to genus).

The Scholastic, genus/species intellectual framework of Gothic architecture has already been noted (among others, by Gottfried Semper and Wilhelm Worringer),[6] and is today a commonplace. In 1951 Erwin Panofsky famously argued that both

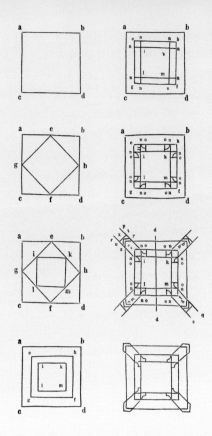

Matthäus Roriczer,
Diagrams showing construction details
of a pinnacle, from *Das Büchlein von
der Fialen Gerechtigkeit*, 1486

Roriczer's was the first illustrated book on architecture in print, but his diagrams still show only geometrical rules for construction (as in the medieval and classical traditions), not repeatable visual models.

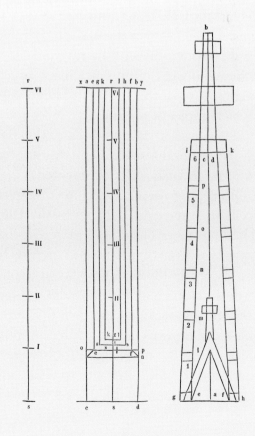

the Gothic and the Scholastic mind cherished the intricacy of subdivisions (for example, in logic, an arborescence of definitions and divisions), and the articulations of both are a game of variations within the same class. From today's vantage point, we should add that the medieval way of building, just like the ancient, classical one, was generative and rule-based – and just like today's Parametricism, it spawned endless variations within given limits.[7]

Classic and medieval Parametricism came to an end with the rise of modern, matrix-based reproductive technologies: from the Renaissance on, printed images replaced verbal rules, and exactly repeatable visual models replaced generative algorithms. So, for example, Vitruvius's and Alberti's capitals were abstract formulas without a standard shape; in the 16th century Vignola's and Palladio's capitals were printed pictures meant for identical replication.

With the Industrial Revolution, mass production spread from pictures to 3D objects, and the modern culture and technologies of identical copies replaced the ancient and medieval culture of scribal and artisanal variations. This is what digital Parametricism stood up against at the close of the 20th century. And this is why it was and still is a revolution: because it produces variations, just like ancient parametricism, but uses machines, just like industrial modernity; and hence can mass-produce variations, which neither antiquity nor modernity ever could. ⌂

NOTES
1. Gilles Deleuze, *Le pli: Leibniz et le baroque*, Editions de Minuit (Paris), 1988; *The Fold: Leibniz and the Baroque*, trans Tom Conley, University of Minnesota Press (Minneapolis, MN), 1993.
2. On the invention of the 'objectile' and the rise of Parametricism in digital design theory, see Mario Carpo (ed), *The Digital Turn in Architecture, 1992–2012*, John Wiley & Sons (Chichester), 2012.
3. Schumacher first used the term in a lecture at the Smart Geometry conference in Munich in 2007, and in print in two contributions to the catalogue of the 11th Venice Architecture Biennale the following year: 'Parametricism as Style – Parametricist Manifesto' and 'Experimentation Within a Long Wave of Innovation', in Aaron Betsky (ed), *Out There: Architecture Beyond Building*, exhibition catalogue, 11th Architecture Biennale, vols 3 and 5, Marsilio Editori and Rizzoli (Venice and New York), 2008. The texts are available online at www.patrikschumacher.com/index.htm. See also Patrik Schumacher, 'Parametricism: A New Global Style for Architecture and Urban Design', in Neil Leach (ed), *D Digital Cities*, July/August (no 4), 2009, pp 14–23.
4. On cybernetics and architecture, see Usman Haque, 'The Architectural Relevance of Gordon Pask', in Lucy Bullivant (ed), *D 4dsocial: Interactive Design Environments*, July/August (no 4), 2007, pp 54-61, with further bibliography.
5. See for example *De Architectura*, III, V, 8, on Ionic columns and architraves. A similar nesting of proportional rules occurs in the case of the layout of the atrium of the private house (*De Arch.*, VI, III, 3), which was recently studied and graphed by Bernard Cache using modern mathematics and digital renderings: Bernard Cache, '*Fortuito supra acanthi radicem: Essai de lecture contemporaine du De Architectura de Vitruve*', unpublished PhD dissertation, University of Paris 1, January 2009.
6. See for example Gottfried Semper, *Der Stil in den technischen und tektonischen Künsten oder praktische Ästhetik*, Verlag für Kunst und Wissenschaft (Frankfurt), 1860, XIX and 509, footnote 1; and Wilhelm Worringer, *Formprobleme der Gotik*, R Pieper (Munich), 1912, translated as: *Form Problems of the Gothic*, GE Stechert (New York), 1920 and GP Putnam's Sons, 1927; as *Form in Gothic*, trans Sir H Read, Schocken (New York), 1957 and 1964; and Tiranti (London), 1957. See Erwin Panofsky, *Gothic Architecture and Scholasticism*, Saint Vincent Archabbey (Latrobe, PA), 1951.
7. See Mario Carpo, 'Parametricism, Digital Scholasticism, and the Decline of Visuality', *The Cornell Journal of Architecture*, 9, 2013, pp 113–19, with further bibliography. On Vitruvius's Parametricism, see the unpublished PhD dissertation by Bernard Cache (cited above). On Gothic Parametricism, see Lars Spuybroek, *The Sympathy of Things: Ruskin and the Ecology of Design*, NAi (Rotterdam), 2011.

With the Industrial Revolution, mass production spread from pictures to 3D objects, and the modern culture and technologies of identical copies replaced the ancient and medieval culture of scribal and artisanal variations. This is what digital Parametricism stood up against at the close of the 20th century.

Mark Burry

Essential Precursors to the Parametricism Manifesto

Antoni Gaudí

Antoni Gaudí,
1:10 inverted (hanging) model
for the Colònia Güell Chapel,
Santa Coloma de Cervelló,
Barcelona,
1898–1906

Scale-inverted (hanging) model for the chapel located just outside Barcelona.

Frei Otto,
Hanging Model,
Leicht bauen, natürlich
gestalten,
Architekturmuseum der
Technischen Universität
München,
Pinakothek der Moderne,
July 2005

opposite: Otto's logical translation of load paths through this 'built diagram' based on the parametrically variable distribution of forces.

and Frei Otto

As Senior Architect to the Basilica of the Sagrada Família in Barcelona, **Mark Burry** has been 'thinking parametrically' for almost his entire career. Here he describes how his longstanding role overseeing the completion of Antoni Gaudí's masterpiece has afforded unique insights into the work of a great geometer and parametric thinker. Burry places the contribution of Gaudí alongside that of Frei Otto – the other eminent 20th-century Proto-Parametricist.

When Patrik Schumacher first unleashed 'Parametricism' on the world in 2008, the principal reason for a largely antagonistic response was the proselytisation of a new style posited as a modus operandi at the expense of the very serious historical and theoretical back-up that was core to the original proposition.[1] Writing myself as someone who had been thinking parametrically for almost my entire professional career commencing in 1979, largely but certainly not exclusively thanks to an early analogue encounter with the efforts to progress Antoni Gaudí's design for the Sagrada Família Basilica in Barcelona, I was not especially bothered by the apparently sudden discovery of 'Parametricism' per se. In Gaudí's 43 years of practice he evolved from historicist to organicist, and ultimately to geometer through his exacting use of geometry – a fusion of intersecting hyperbolic paraboloids with hyperboloids of revolution: parametrically variable flexible architectural design by any definition. With this hands-on introduction to Gaudí's parametric thinking extending over decades I considered that the style argument was therefore a rather unfortunate distraction, taking the creative mind away from the principal core issue – thinking and acting parametrically.

As the ensuing kerfuffle has matured towards 'Parametricism 2.0', Schumacher's announcement of the new style as a manifesto seven years ago, intentionally or otherwise a debate on a crucial dimension of computationally influenced architecture was initiated that might otherwise have been quickly passed by were Parametricism situated merely as a methodological commentary on a particular approach to design. As a result of that original and unexpected position statement, we now have a generation of emerging architects who have been extraordinarily sensitised to the fundamental nature of design parameters, and the way that self-consciously aware digital design computation through parametrically variable inputs can be welcomed as a driver for a far greater sophistication within the studio.

Personally I favour any deliberate design process that keeps digital agency firmly under the control of the architect, and at some distance ahead of any careless deployment of someone else's algorithm, or the embrace of the accident and other related happenstances.[2] It is surely essential that architects make good use of the manifesto as a provocation medium, and the announcement of Parametricism was one of the first wide-reaching manifestos of this scale possibly since Archigram

GMP Architekten,
Stuttgart Airport Terminal 1,
Stuttgart,
1991

The tree-like structure of the aiport terminal interior demonstrates the portability of robust ideas based on parametric variability.

Rolf Gutbrod, Frei Otto,
BuroHappold and
Ove Arup and Partners,
Kings Office,
Council of Ministers,
Majlis al Shura,
Riyadh,
Saudi Arabia,
1979

Model showing the support pillars of the six-angle gridshell of this unbuilt proposal.

et al in the 1960s. By being declared a 'style', Parametricism has oxygenated contemporary architectural fixation beyond 'starchitecture' with the necessary polemical oomph to get everyone sharpening their metaphorical pen nibs if not their swords. The nature of the manifesto as a catalyst to push matters forward segues neatly into a dissection of Theo van Doesburg's 'Towards a Plastic Architecture' manifesto of 1924 that aligns so closely to the subsequent introduction of computational design into contemporary architecture.[3]

In a nutshell, Van Doesburg calls for a parametrically variable ('plastic') architecture in all but name. In Proposition 1 he rails against style: 'Instead of taking as a model earlier types of style and, in so doing, imitating earlier styles, it is necessary to pose the problem of architecture completely afresh.' In Proposition 2 he elaborates: 'The new architecture is elementary, that is, it is developed from the elements of building, in the widest sense. These elements, such as function, mass, plane, time, space, light, colour, material, etc., are at the same time elements of plasticism.' Here we might substitute the term 'elements' with 'variables'. Proposition 9 contends: 'Space and time. The new architecture takes account not only of space, but also of time as an accent of architecture. The unity

of time and space gives the appearance of architecture a new and completely plastic aspect (four-dimensional temporal and spatial plastic aspects).'

The version of Van Doesburg's manifesto appearing in Ulrich Conrads's 1970 collation of *Programs and Manifestoes on 20th-Century Architecture* includes the following extract: 'For this purpose Euclidean mathematics will be of no further use — but with the aid of calculation that is non-Euclidean and takes into account the four dimensions everything will be very easy.'[4] 'Easy' might not be the term that first springs to mind to any adept in today's sophisticated parametric software, but it is certainly easier now than it would have been for first Antoni Gaudí and subsequently Frei Otto with their manually executed empirical evaluations of gravity-affected form, which fascinatingly presage current preoccupations.

Antoni Gaudí and Frei Otto: Proto-Parametricists

Gaudí's mid-career designs (around 1900 to 1914) bear important similarities to the work emerging from Otto's studio (especially during the 1960s and 1970s), particularly in the way both used 'flexible models' to work with 'freeform'.

We now have a generation of emerging architects who have been extraordinarily sensitised to the fundamental nature of design parameters

Reconstruction of Gaudí's hanging model for the Colònia Güell Chapel, Sagrada Família Basilica Museum, Barcelona, 1980s

This model, painstakingly reproduced by Jos Tomlow and team at 1:15 scale, provided many valuable insights into Gaudí's working methodology for this project.

They were inspired to call on gravity, one of nature's ultimate parametric design inputs, to inform rather than plan architectural form as an essential physical determinant within the design process. In terms of the Van Doesburg manifesto, gravity is a fourth-dimensional non-Euclidean parameter. The execution of Gaudí's and Otto's experiments using hanging models can be argued to be a physical call on the ultimate truth: architectural volume following the shape that gravity imposes on materials in use.

However, along every design trajectory that takes idea through to artefact there are important differences between ambition and outcome, for example the problem of the fully executed 'equilibrated design' that has veered off in a different direction than that originally 'formed' (as opposed to planned) through the hanging models. The equilibrated design is an absolute condition – something that engineers might strive for, but architects might be wary of.

Such a logical path to a design might need to be tracked differently should the design change through the imposition of competing parameters. This so-called Pareto optimisation and quest for effective parametric trade-offs is the enemy of the absolute conditions of parametric design. The significance of the similarities between Gaudí and Otto as predigital precursors for designing parametrically counters any claim that Parametricism, in itself, is merely a contemporary digital

condition. The similarities as well as the differences between the two architects are evidence of alternative flexibilities of the flexible model. Seen in this light, any concerns that parametric inputs are in fact unfriendly and non-negotiable design constraints – a design straightjacket – may be challenged without hiding behind a label and a digital design computation mask.

Dangerous Liaisons? (Or Architectural Practice Not as We Have Traditionally Understood It to Be?)

Is Parametricism 2.0 a dangerous step down the road towards the destruction of the profession of architecture, or is it simply architectural practice as we know it that is at risk?

By extending the parametric inputs of architectural design to include environmental, political, social, cultural, practical, economic, theoretical, philosophical and behavioural parameters (this is not an exclusive list by any means), for the first time the architect can act as the equivalent of the operatic impresario. The range and potential impact of big data inputs necessarily displaces the architect from any earnest belief that they can continue to assume the role of sole design author.

What makes both Gaudí and Otto such exciting players in the Parametricism debate is the evidence of expanded design horizons that their experimental intensity reveals. Both gift us their deep understanding of and commitment to the rich matrix that structure and materials make together with the

Frei Otto and Günther Behnisch,
Olympic Stadium,
Munich,
1972

The design strategy for the stadium sits somewhere between Gaudí's hanging model for a chapel, and the advanced high-tech options of today, demonstrating the portability of parametric approaches to translating ideas into outcomes.

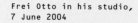

Frei Otto in his studio,
7 June 2004

Abundant evidence of Otto's experimentation on view in his studio. Empirical investigation within a fully resolved intellectual framework characterised Otto's design approach.

physical and biotechnical foundations of the natural world – at both macro- and microscopic levels. What they achieved as essential precursor agents for a digitally driven Parametricism should help convince latter-day fence-sitters that the wonderful new world of flexible design strategies, still on the cusp of fully emerging, will greatly extend their repertoire. Working parametrically across the full gamut of inputs there are abundant opportunities to enrich individual practice. To do so architects will have to find a way to embrace a computationally mediated dialogue by contributing a much broader range of parametric variables to the mix drawn from experts who are not necessarily fellow architects.

'Embrace' is the operative word here: thinking and creating parametrically will need to scale-up radically to the urban scale. Parametric thinking spans the minute scale and the mega. Although still out of the reach of our existing technology, we are nevertheless not so far away from the advent of the computational power necessary to convert the analytical outputs from 'big data' into meaningful design inputs. Directly linking data outputs to parametric inputs will help meet requirements for future megacities being all that they could be as positive places fit for all human aspirations and activity. This might have been beyond the scope of Gaudí and Otto given their respective historical, cultural and technical contexts, but they signal that it is surely ours to embrace tomorrow if not quite today. ∆

Notes
1. Patrik Schumacher, 'Parametricism as Style – Parametricist Manifesto', presented and discussed at the Dark Side Club, 11th Architecture Biennale, Venice, 2008: www.patrikschumacher.com/Texts/Parametricism%20as%20Style.htm. See also Karen Cilento, 'Parametricist Manifesto/Patrik Schumacher', ArchDaily, 16 June 2010: www.archdaily.com/64581/parametricist-manifesto-patrik-schumacher/ and Patrik Schumacher, 'Parametricism: A New Global Style for Architecture and Urban Design', in Neil Leach (ed), ∆ Digital Cities, July/August (no 4), 2009, pp 14–23.
2. Mark Burry, 'Gaudi, Teratology and Kinship', in Stephen Perrella (ed), ∆ Hypersurface Architecture, May/June (no 3), 1998 pp 38-43.
3. Theo van Doesburg, 'Tot een Beeldende Architectuur' (Towards a Plastic Architecture), De Stijl, 6 (6–7), 1924, pp 78–83.
4. Theodore van Doesburg, extracted from Proposition 9 of 'Towards a Plastic Architecture', 1924, in Ulrich Conrads, Programs and Manifestoes on 20th-Century Architecture, MIT Press (Cambridge, MA), 1970, p 79.

Antoni Gaudí,
Colònia Güell Chapel,
Barcelona,
1898–1914

left: Detail of the hyperbolic paraboloids forming the porch ceiling above the crypt entrance. Hyperbolic paraboloids are infinitely parametrically variable surfaces and offer significant constructional advantages through their generation from straight lines as well as their structural efficiency. For the many quadrilateral mesh elements emerging from the hanging model the hyperbolic paraboloid was the obvious solution for four conjoined nonplanar straight edges emerging from the string network that formed the flexible hanging model.

bottom: Gaudí used naturally occurring hexagonal basalt prisms from Northern Catalunya for the principal columns. Notwithstanding the calculations made through the hanging model he nevertheless intervened during the making of the building – apparently requesting that the stonemasons make scarf cuts where the columns meet their bases.

Theodore Spyropoulos

Behavioural Complexity

Minimaforms, Museum of
Light, Hungarian Museum
of Architecture and Foto-
Muzeum, Budapest, 2014

The proposal experiments with
illumination, constructing veils of
translucency that create an urban and
landscape intervention as a symbolic
gateway for the city.

Constructing Frameworks for Human–Machine Ecologies

Founded by Patrik Schumacher and Brett Steele in 1997, the Architectural Association Design Research Laboratory (AADRL) Master's programme, based at the AA in London, provides an important research base for Parametricism. The current Director of AADRL, **Theodore Spyropoulos,** continues to push the boundaries of advanced computing and machine intelligence. Here he describes the work that he has undertaken at the AA and through his practice Minimaforms into adaptive ecologies that employ responsive machine learning to enable spatial transformations.

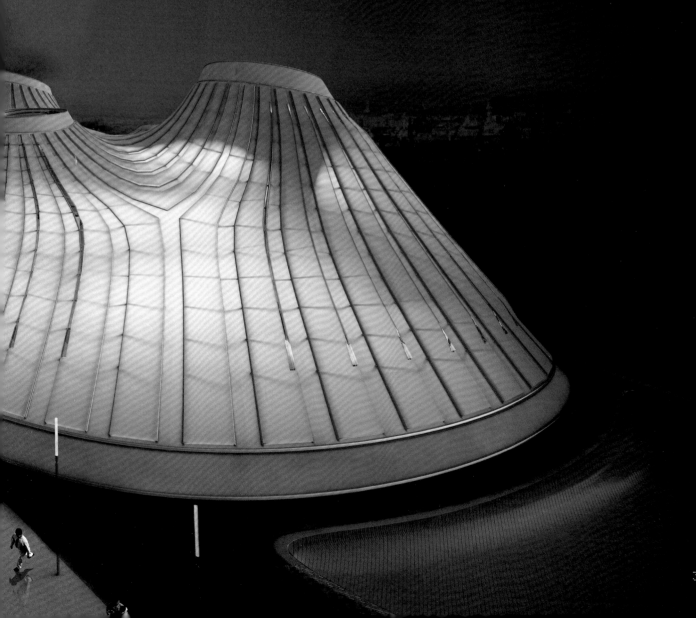

It's going to be harder to distinguish: what is alive and what is a machine ... And that boundary may start to become meaningless.
– Rodney Brooks, in *Fast, Cheap & Out of Control*, documentary film (director Errol Morris), 1997[1]

In 1968, Austrian radical architect Hans Hollein proclaimed 'Alles ist Architektur' (Everything is Architecture). Published originally as a manifesto that appeared in the journal *Bau*,[2] it was a provocation that reflected a heightened awareness of the limitations of traditional definitions of architecture in favour of an understanding of design as an experimental vehicle for the construction of new forms of communication. Beyond building, Hollein stated:

> A true architecture of our time will have to redefine itself and expand its means. Many areas outside of traditional building will enter the realm of architecture, as architecture and 'architects' will have to enter new fields. All are architects. Everything is architecture.[3]

Architecture in an expanded field of experimentation resonates with great magnitude today as we live in an age where science fiction has become fact. Our contemporary age is as radical as ever with change, latency and uncertainty being the new norm. The once confortable and understood historical models of the past have proven limited in their capacity to engage and address the complexities of the contemporary condition. As we live in ever-evolving information-rich environments, the question is how architecture can actively participate.

TOWARDS A BEHAVIOURAL MODEL FOR ARCHITECTURE

Conceiving architecture as an ecology of interacting systems moves the fixed and finite tendencies of the past towards spatial environments that are adaptive, emotive and behavioural. Environments within this framework are attempts to construct interaction scenarios that enable agency, curiosity and play, forging intimate exchanges that are participatory, emotive and evolving over time. Interaction understood as the evolving relationships between things allows a generative and time-based framework to explore space as a model of interfacing that shifts the tendencies of passive occupancy towards an active and evolving ecology of interacting agents.

The approach proposed here is illustrated in the work of architecture and design studio Minimaforms and the research it is developing at the Architectural Association Design Research Lab (AADRL) in London. Here, architecture moves away from known models that reinforce habitual responses within the discipline, towards

Minimaforms (Theodore Spyropoulos) with Krzysztof Wodiczko, Vehicle (War Veterans) Prototype, 2006–10

The vehicle amplifies the built environment through its mobility and embedded communication instruments. An extension of the veteran, it animates and projects their personal stories and testimonies within public spaces.

Minimaforms,
Emotive City,
'FutureFest',
London,
2015

The project, commissioned by the Nesta Innovation Department, explored a model that enables everyday emotive interactions of the public and social scenarios to influence how a city is structured.

Minimaforms,
Brunel Gateway,
Uxbridge, UK,
2007-09

Brunel Gateway is a seeing machine, deployed as an open-cell network of operable convex and concave lenses that amplify and collapse the experiential relationships between users and their context.

an understanding of adaptive ecologies that are active agents for communication and exploration. Architecture within this context is explored as a medium for spatial interfacing. Design is thus considered as durational, real-time and anticipatory, exploring human–machine, machine–machine and human–human communication.

PARTICIPANTS AS PERFORMERS

Within this behavioural discourse, architecture is understood as an open framework. As ecologies of interaction, spatial environments serve as a stimulus for participation. Participatory models offer dynamic and intuitive relationships between the environment, observers and performers within the system, and it is through such models for interaction that it becomes apparent that architecture can serve as a host to enable scenario-based exchanges that amplify space as an interface for communication.

In principle, this communication can be human or non-human. Human agency can be used to explore new forms of communication that challenge conventional systemic approaches of finite programming and control. The architecture proposed is active, anticipatory and adaptive through continuous exchanges that are real-time and behaviour based. Architecture is here understood to have agency; to sense, to learn, to stimulate, to understand and to get bored.

Through direct experience, participants evolve their novel relations into enquiry and constructive understanding. This dialogue between things that emerge through curiosity and play can exhibit collective tendencies that can be experienced as intelligent. Intelligence, as Dr Ranulph Glanville reminds us in his 2001 paper 'An Intelligent Architecture':

> is experienced by us from individual instances we have observed: that is, we observe, we generalize (find pattern) and we create the concept of intelligence, which we then both modify as we go, and allow to determine whether various acts and behaviors we observe are intelligent or not.[4]

The move towards a spatial and conversational model of interaction pursues a definition of an intelligent architecture in the spirit that Glanville has defined: 'Intelligence depends on the interface of our interaction.'[5] The challenge is therefore to construct environments that are shared between participants and allow for complex interactions to arise through human agency and the observed agency of these interactions. Environments where the focus is on behavioural features that afford conversation-rich exchanges between participant and system, participant with other participants, and/or systems with other systems. This evolving framework of relationships demands that design systems have the capacity to understand and learn through interaction.

Beyond conventional models that are reactive in their definition of interaction, architecture aims to move towards deeper levels of understanding that are lifelike, machine learned and emotively communicated. Systemic evolutionary methods are enabled through the everyday, where behaviour is not relegated to a generative process in the design phase; rather it is an architecture of the now, constantly building models of and for communication. This capacity allows architecture to truly evolve with and challenge us.

BEYOND CONTROL: STEPS TOWARDS AN ECOLOGY OF INTERACTIVE THINGS

Control within systems in the behavioural approach to architecture illustrated here would be relational and collective, as summarised succinctly by second-order cybernetician Gordon Pask when he states:

> When learning to control or to solve problems man necessarily conceptualizes and abstracts … the human environment is interpreted at various levels in a hierarchy of abstraction. These propensities are at the root of curiosity and assimilation of knowledge. They impel man to explore, discover and explain his inanimate surroundings.[6]

Unlike the formal methods of abstraction of the past that simplified the world of operation, the work of Minimaforms problematises and delves into the rich complexities that spatial practice enables. Unlike arguments of animate form and key framed simulation spaces that form illustrative, process-driven representations of the world, it examines time as a medium of awareness and communication. Behavioural complexity engages new forms of interaction that are social, material and environmental. The model moves away from forms of representation towards a model of demonstration that is motivated by creating multiple possibilities rather than singular solution spaces. The goal is to construct a behavioural synthesis where complexity resides in the relationships between things, rather than as attributes to things.

Two Minimaforms projects in particular may assist in further articulating this shared and evolving exchange. *Memory Cloud*, which was performed in Trafalgar Square, London, in 2008 and at the Detroit Institute of Arts (DIA), Michigan, in 2010, explored architecture as an atmosphere by constructing an environment that was ephemeral and collective, offering a participatory model enacted with the public space as pure communication. Petting Zoo, first installed as part of the 'Naturalizing Architecture' exhibition at the Frac Centre, Orléans, France, in 2013 and most recently at the Barbican's 'Digital Revolution' in London, offers a model for engaged artificially intelligent emotive robotic agency.

FROM ATMOSPHERES TO ROBOTICS

Based on one of the oldest forms of visual communication – the ancient practice of smoke signals – fused with contemporary mediums, *Memory Cloud* constructed a dynamic hybrid space that communicated personal statements as part of an evolving text, animating the built environment through conversation. Interaction was facilitated through mobile phones, creating an open, personal and accessible platform for collective participation. The public spaces were thus transformed into dynamic stages of communication, the shared and collective nature of which constructed an evolving and complex set of relationships that enabled sustained novelty and crowd-based cooperative interaction.

The power of this ephemeral work to enact change through its ability to bring communities together and use the city as a medium of communication was especially evident in Detroit. Performed over three days, it here served as the basis of a city initiative that took the form of a light biennale named DLECTRICITY that continues to explore the city as a canvas for collective expression.

Petting Zoo is a speculative robotic environment populated by artificially intelligent creatures that, through a real-time camera-tracking system that can detect the presence of people, their gestures and activities, have the capacity to process data from which they can learn and explore different behaviours through interaction with participants.

The power of this ephemeral work to enact change through its ability to bring communities together and use the city as a medium of communication was especially evident in Detroit.

This evolutionary model for design
explores high populations of
interacting agents that have
the capacity to be self-aware,
to self-structure and assemble.

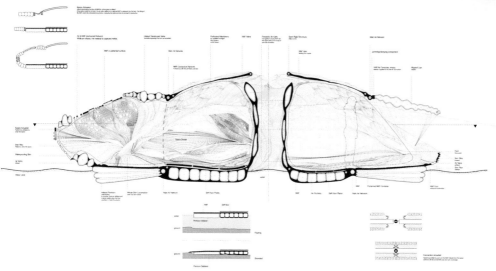

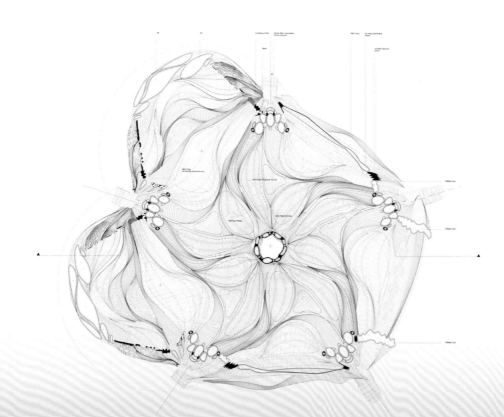

AADRL Spyropoulos
Design Lab (students:
Antonios Thodis,
Camilla Degli Esposti,
Ilya Pereyaslavtsev
and Agata Banaszek),
Project OWO,
Architectural
Association Design
Research Lab, London,
2015

opposite top: Self-assembled
mobility prototypes were
developed through evolving
organisational body plans. These
self-aware systems are mobile
and construct self-assembled
and self-structured architectures.

AADRL Spyropoulos
Design Lab (students:
Miguel Miranda, Said
Fahim Mohammadi,
Katharina Penner and
Yifan Zhang), Project
SoProto, Architectural
Association Design
Research Lab, London,
2011

opposite middle and bottom:
The research explored a soft
body architecture that constructs
adaptive models of mobility.
The material circulation system
proposed exploited the use of
non-Newtonian fluids to create
a reactive spatial environment
through its material agency.

Within this immersive installation, which is travelling to various locations for a period of five years, interaction with the lifelike attributes of these 'pets' fosters human curiosity and play, forging intimate exchanges that are emotive and sensorial, evolve over time and enable communication between people and their environment. Social and synthetic forms of systemic interactions with the public in turn allow the pets to exhibit lifelike features and personalities. They stimulate participation with users and other pets within the population through animate behaviours communicated via visual, haptic and aural means. *Petting Zoo* is thus an exploration of artificial intelligence that prompts us to think about how we can co-evolve and inhabit our future human–machine environments. Moving beyond robotics as merely tools of production, it examines the emotive and behavioural features of our engagement with them and with each other.

EVOLVING TAXONOMIES

Built and physical architecture, freed from the technological limitations of the past, will more intensely work with spatial qualities as well as with psychological ones.
— Hans Hollein, 'Alles ist Architektur' (Everything is Architecture), *Bau: Magazine for Architecture and Town Planning*, 1/2, 1968, p 2[7]

In addition to the human-to-human and human-to-machine interactions described above, machine-to-machine interactions within adaptive machine ecologies are evolutionary and engage a world of behavioural practice that moves beyond top-down and bottom-up computational logic. These ecologies consist of families of high-population agents which construct fitness criteria by distributing genetic algorithmic processes that inform their morphological and neurological control systems.

This competitive digital breeding environment was illustrated, for example, in the seminal papers on the subject by the computer graphics artist and researcher Karl Simms in the mid-1990s.[8] Here, organisation is understood through body plan generation that at a local level engages immediate goals; for example, first-order organisational strategies for mobility. Rather than privileging prescriptive models, the genetic pool evolves and tests relational and population-dependent organisations that aim to perform through locomotion. This process affords a plurality of plausible design solutions, performing as a body or creature for a certain duration before other, higher-order goals emerge.

The aim of this process is to evolve creatures that are self-aware and have autonomy of control to allow each organisation to understand itself and, in the example above, learn to move. The research in this area by Minimaforms and the AADRL examines taxonomies that evolve over time, creating possibilities to explore architecture in continual formation. Through the creations of these body plans, complexity emerges as adaptive responses to evolving and latent pressures. This approach allows families of interacting agents to construct ecologies of relational exchange. Behavioural complexities are enabled as the agents may act independently or create 'super bodies', affording a dynamic examination of relational and goal-oriented interactions that emerge out of scenario-based playpens.

This evolutionary model for design explores high populations of interacting agents that have the capacity to be self-aware, to self-structure and assemble. Environmental conditioning, machine learning and collective building expand conceptions of architecture beyond finite forms of production and realisation, towards an adaptive model that evolves with human exchange. Enabled through programmable matter, actuated soft robotics and embedded sensing technologies, behavioural complexity offers new terms of reference for architecture. This architecture will engage us, challenge us and enable new species and taxonomies of proto human-machine ecologies. We are only just scratching the surface. ⌂

NOTES
1. Rodney Brooks, in *Fast, Cheap & Out of Control*, documentary film directed by Errol Morris, Sony Pictures Classics, 1997.
2. Hans Hollein, 'Alles ist Architektur', *Bau: Magazine for Architecture and Town Planning*, 1/2, 1968, available at www.ica.org.uk/sites/default/files/Press%20Release%20Everything%20is%20Architecture.pdf.
3. *Ibid*, p 3.
4. Ranulph Glanville, 'An Intelligent Architecture', *Convergence: The International Journal of Research into New Media Technologies*, 7 (2), June 2001, p 2.
5. *Ibid*, p 8.
6. Gordon Pask, 'A Comment, a Case History and a Plan', in Jasia Reichardt (ed), *Cybernetic Art and Ideas*, Studio Vista (London), 1971, p 76.
7. Hans Hollein, *op cit*, p 2.
8. See Karl Sims, 'Evolving Virtual Creatures', *Siggraph '94: Proceedings of the 21st Annual Conference on Computer Graphics and Interactive Techniques*, July 1994, pp 15–22, and Karl Sims, 'Evolving 3D Morphology and Behavior in Competition', in Rodney Brooks and Pattie Maes (eds), *Artificial Life IV: Proceedings of the Fourth International Workshop on the Synthesis and Simulation of Living Systems*, MIT Press (Cambridge, MA), 1994, pp 28–39.

UPGRADI
COMPUTA
DESIGN

Shajay Bhooshan

NG
TIONAL

Zaha Hadid Architects,
Mathematics Gallery,
Science Museum,
London,
due for completion 2016

The competition-winning
design was created using
multiple algorithms and design
technologies developed over
many years by ZHACODE and
its collaborators.

Shajay Bhooshan heads up the computation and design ZHACODE group at Zaha Hadid Architects (ZHA) and is a course master at the Architectural Association Design Research Laboratory (AADRL). Here he argues that Parametricism 2.0 has a vital role to play in the progressing of computational design. Assimilating the exploratory developments of the last 15 years, he asserts how the next phase of Parametricism will enable a further consolidation and evolution of digital practices.

Having recently marked the centenary of the creation of Le Corbusier's influential set of abstract and prototypical architectural principals, *Maison dom-ino* (1914–15), it is worth considering one of its principal contributions: the way that it embraced technological confidence and the optimism of the time within an architectural discourse. It also recalls the techno-centric histories penned by Sigfried Giedion[1] during the same period, and their wider influence. Le Corbusier's invention and Giedion's work were significant in terms of both their direct dissemination of and indirect influences on the emerging modern architectural cultures of the developing world. Parametricism,[2] although often debated for its merits and demerits as an architectural style, endeavours to similarly unify disparate efforts in computational design across the globe and to incorporate technological advances within its theoretical discourse, all of which is conducive to the systemic upgrading of computational practice within architectural design.

Ever since the revolutionary invention of Ivan Sutherland's Sketchpad as the first computer-aided design (CAD) software in 1963, architecture has certainly been a forerunner among design disciplines in adopting the use of the computer. The article here, however, focuses on a contemporary history of computational design over the last 15 years. In *Animate Form*,[3] his 1999 article and book by the same name, Greg Lynn made a now-famous call to architects to rethink their relation to computer software and to retool themselves. Architects have since worked vigorously in doing exactly that. In the process, architecture has witnessed exploratory phases of the discovery of possibilities, and exploitative phases of invention in the use of computer software and physical computing. Parametricism has sought to recognise both, as periods where either extraordinary diagrams or ordinary diagrams are privileged.[4]

These two diagrams types are distinct: in the former, the operative means and protocols to transform ideas into architectural production are not clearly known, while in the latter they are. The argument here is that the discipline and profession of architecture currently exhibits features that are consistent with an exploitative phase of consolidation where the ordinary diagram is more prevalent. This is what we might call 'Parametricism 2.0'. Such a focused endeavour on assimilating and refining the findings mined during the prior exploratory phase is necessary for the systemic evolution of computational capabilities, as can be discerned in the following aspects for contemporary computational design practice.

INCREASED INTERDISCIPLINARY COLLABORATION

In his book *Impossibility*,[5] John Barrow noted that disciplines gearing to deliver sustained growth and societal contributions are characterised by large collaborative projects. This is certainly true in architecture today, as even a cursory survey of professional practice will reveal. Opportunities for collaboration and co-authorship of the built environment are enabled by the sharing of computational tools, algorithms and software across the principal participants of the design process: architects, engineers and manufacturers. The ubiquitous uptake of software platforms such as Grasshopper®,[6] and its forerunner, Generative Components™,[7] are cases in point. Recent forays by large informational companies such as Google

with their data-rich platforms including Flux™,[8] and the more foundational offerings of SketchUp™, also hint at the coming future of collaborative data- and algorithm-driven architecture. Such increased collaboration is also mirrored in the authorship of research papers in scientific journals and books. Collaboration is promoting the unearthing of huge repositories of interesting areas of scientific research and problems to be solved. Along with the attendant potential opportunities of business, this has engendered mathematicians such as Helmut Pottmann, and computer scientists such as Mark Pauly, to contribute significantly to the rapidly evolving field of architectural geometry and computational understanding. Once the exclusive domain of computer scientists, the authoritative conferences of SIGGRAPH and Eurographics now routinely feature tracks related to architectural geometry and construction research.[9] Likewise, while structural engineering traditionally dominated conferences such as IASS, these now increasingly present contributions from architects. Reciprocally, where architecture previously monopolised conferences and associated journals such as SmartGeometry, ACADIA and CAADRIA, they now include diverse offerings from roboticists, engineers and geometers. Lastly, increases in architectural domain-specific knowledge are evident in the emergence of conferences and publications such as Advances in Architectural Geometry (AAG), the Design Modelling Symposium (DMS) and Robotic Fabrication in Architecture, Art and Design (Rob|Arch).

ARCHITECTURE has witnessed exploratory phases of the discovery of possibilities, and exploitative phases of invention in the use of computer software and physical computing.

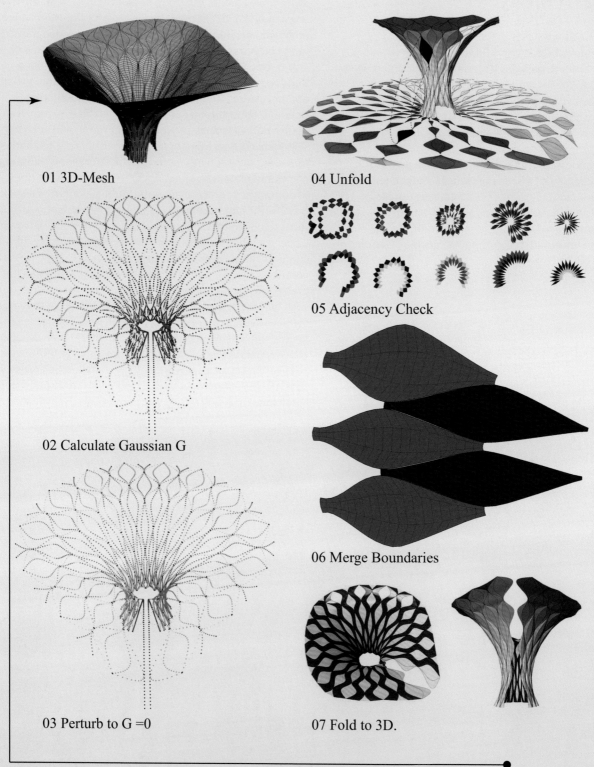

01 3D-Mesh

02 Calculate Gaussian G

03 Perturb to G =0

04 Unfold

05 Adjacency Check

06 Merge Boundaries

07 Fold to 3D.

Multi-stage workflow for the design of 500 panels.

Zaha Hadid Architects,
Arum digital workflow,
Venice Architecture Biennale,
2012

Custom digital design workflow developed
by ZHACODE for the *Arum* installation
designed to enable a fluid collaboration
between the architects, engineers
BuroHappold and manufacturer RoboFold.

HISTORIC CONTINUUM OF METHODS

An increasing desire to seek a historic continuum as opposed to radical jettison of historical ideas and methods is evidenced in the rediscovery of the foundations laid by past masters and its proactive development; be it the extension of and making accessible the structural genius of Frei Otto, Antoni Gaudí and others by Sigrid Adriaenssens, Philippe Block, Diederik Veenendaal and Chris Williams,[10] the appropriation of the evolutionary computation of John Holland and John Frazer, the shape grammars of George Stiny and so on. It is particularly poignant to note that contemporary research in architectural computing shares a renewed interest in the pioneering work of architects and engineers from the 1960s and 1970s as opposed to the more immediate past of Postmodern architecture. As such, computational researchers – both young and established – are divining the computational work from that period of engineers and architects at the Institute for Lightweight Structures (ILEK) at the University of Stuttgart; the seminal theoretical framework of descriptions, predictions and evaluations from Lionel March and others from the University of Cambridge that was recorded in March's book *The Architecture of Form* (1976);[11] the structural formalism of Félix Candela and Pier Luigi Nervi; and the work of Seymour Papert and MIT's Architecture Machine Group. Extensive contributions by Mark Burry in making the geometric genius of Antoni Gaudí more widely accessible cannot go unmentioned in this context.

Zaha Hadid Architects,
Undisclosed project and location,
2012

above and right: The design and tectonic articulation of the project was a result of research in digital design methods and prototypes developed by ZHACODE over several years, particularly regarding the form-finding of structurally sound shapes, their efficient manufacture and the tectonic articulation of their structural performance.

Contemporary RESEARCH in architectural computing shares a renewed interest in the pioneering work of architects and engineers from the 1960s and 1970s.

SYSTEMIC GENERATION AND DISSEMINATION OF DESIGN RESEARCH AND SCIENTIFIC KNOWLEDGE

The last decade and a half has also seen the emergence of domain-specific education and research groups such as the Institute for Computational Design (ICD) at the University of Stuttgart (see pp 76–83), the Block Research Group (BRG) and Gramazio Kohler Research at ETH Zurich (see pp 68–75), and the Centre for Information Technology and Architecture (CITA) at the Royal Danish Academy of Fine Arts in Copenhagen. These are synergetic with the more domain-general antecedents such as the Design Research Laboratory at the Architectural Association (AADRL) in London and the Southern California Institute of Architecture (SCI-Arc) in Los Angeles. Such synergy, along with advancement in the support apparatus of research grants, symposia, conferences and publications is enabling a systemic upgrading of scientific methods of research and practice.[12] The pioneering efforts of the AADRL should be particularly noted in this aspect; in its 20 years of existence, it has been a tireless developer of interdisciplinary and collaborative team-based design research. Apart from serving as a blueprint for several subsequent educational institutions, its communal and creative environs have propelled several generations of architects to pursue architectural research within a scientific paradigm without eschewing the more weathered socioeconomic concerns of the profession.

Zaha Hadid Architects,
Research prototype for the use of curved-crease-folded moulds to construct funicular skeletons, Chennai, India, 2014

This research prototype, built as part of the Architectural Association (AA) Visiting School programme, was a proof-of-concept demonstrator of ZHACODE's continued R&D into funicular structures (with the Block Research Group), and their efficient production using curve-crease folded metallic moulds (with Paul Shepherd and Paul Richens of the University of Bath).

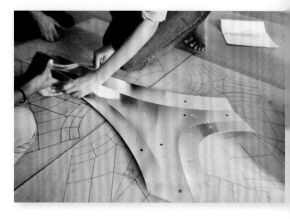

SYMBIOSIS BETWEEN
ACADEMIA AND PRACTICE

We can also sense an increase in the fluid exchange of people, projects and information between leading academic institutions and professional architectural practices. Commercial software and technology vendors such as Autodesk, Bentley Systems, Dassault Systèmes and McNeel are also salient partners in this exchange. At Zaha Hadid Architects this has meant a mutually beneficial relationship between the firm's pedagogical activities in its proving grounds of the AADRL and Masterclass at the University of Applied Arts Vienna, and the discursive and professional practices of the company. The work of Christian Derix and others from Aedas and their academic affiliations at the University of East London is another example of a fruitful marriage. The relationships of Chris Williams[13] and colleagues at the University of Bath with, for example, BuroHappold Engineering and Foster + Partners, are another prominent collaboration. Computational practitioners such as Stylianos Dritsas (previously at Kohn Pedersen Fox Associates), Sawako Kaijima and Panagiotis Michalatos (both previously with Adams Kara Taylor structural engineers) and others who started their careers in professional practices now occupy prominent academic positions at the Singapore University of Technology and Design (SUTD) and Harvard University Graduate School of Design (GSD).

Lastly, following on from the pioneering contributions of Hugh Whitehead at Foster + Partners's Specialist Modelling Group, Neil Katz at SOM's Blackbox Studio, Shrikant Sharma as head of BuroHappold's SMART Solutions team, and Dennis Shelden at Gehry Technologies, there has been a prolific growth of in-house computational teams in other practices. Although not conceived as a specialist knowledge group, ZHACODE has also aimed to contribute to the pedagogic and discursive practices of Zaha Hadid Architects. The aim is to foster collaborative associations with specialist knowledge groups from other disciplines, and particularly fruitful ones have already been established with the Block Research Group, University of Bath and Autodesk Research.

Zaha Hadid Architects,
3D-printed chair prototype,
2014

Below and overleaf: This collaboration between ZHACODE and Stratasys Inc required the development of a custom workflow with repeated iteration between design and structural analysis, and utilises innovative material-saving technology developed by Altair Technologies.

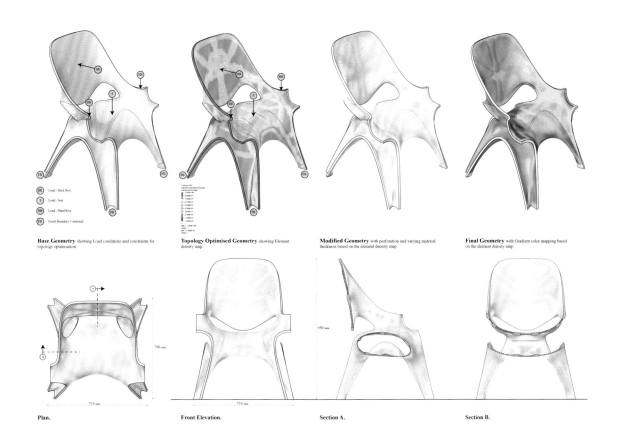

Base Geometry showing Load conditions and constraints for topology optimisation.

Topology Optimised Geometry showing Element density map.

Modified Geometry with perforation and varying material thickness based on the element density map.

Final Geometry with Gradient color mapping based on the element density map.

Plan.

Front Elevation.

Section A.

Section B.

ARCHITECTURE is en route
to deliver habitats that
parallel those of nature.

Zaha Hadid Architects,
3D-printed chair prototype,
2014

CONTINUED EVOLUTION

As briefly outlined in this synoptic, techno-centric history of the last 15 years, the foundations for the sustained upgrading and evolution of architectural computing and scientific methods of research and practice have been laid. This is already having a profound influence on architectural morphology and its genesis based on its sound structural principles, the enhancement of performative aspects with respect to the environment and energy, efficient manufacture and, ultimately, for the comfortable and harmonious occupation and navigation by people. This augurs well for a future with a mutually beneficial relation between science and architecture. In the last 45 years, such a bidirectional relationship between the natural sciences and computer science has led to a prolific growth of innovation in both disciplines.[14] With a similar coupling of rapid advancements in computational technologies, robotic manufacture and data-rich cultures with the accrued wisdom of built traditions, architecture is en route to deliver habitats that parallel those of nature. ⧄

Notes
1. Sigfried Giedion, *Space, Time and Architecture*, Harvard University Press (Cambridge, MA), 1967.
2. Patrik Schumacher, 'Parametricism : A New Global Style for Architecture and Urban Design', in Neil Leach (ed), ⧄ *Digital Cities*, July/August (no 4), 2009, pp 14–23.
3. Greg Lynn, *Animate Form*, Princeton Architectural Press (New York), 1999.
4. Patrik Schumacher, *The Autopoiesis of Architecture, Vol I: A New Framework for Architecture*, John Wiley & Sons (Chichester), 2011.
5. John Barrow, *Impossibility*, Oxford University Press (New York), 1998.
6. Grasshopper is a visual programming platform developed by McNeel Associates.
7. The Generative Components programming platform was developed by Bentley systems and was a pioneering attempt in architectural computing to introduce explicit control of the parameters that generate geometry.
8. Flux is a provider of collaborative design software that spun-out of Google X. It aims to incorporate data regarding planning regulations and environmental simulations within the design process.
9. In this regard, Philippe Block and his collaborators at the Block Research Group (BRG) at ETH Zurich are a very rare and prominent example of architectural papers being accepted into SIGGRAPH. Block currently has three seminal contributions to the conference and journal. (See also his article on pp 68–75 of this issue.)
10. Sigrid Adriaenssens, Philippe Block, Diederik Veenendaal and Chris Williams (eds), *Shell Structures for Architecture: Form Finding and Optimization*, Routledge (London), 2014.
11. Lionel March, *The Architecture of Form*, Cambridge University Press (Cambridge), 1976.
12. In this context, it would be worth mentioning the recent and large collaborative research-and-practice networks of Innochain in Europe and the National Centre of Competence in Research's Digital Fabrication in Switzerland.
13. Chris Williams was the engineer for the seminal roof project over the Great Court of London's British Museum where he produced custom software specifically to develop its (structural) design.
14. See 'Steering the Future of Computing', *Nature*, 440 (73), March 2006, pp 383–580.

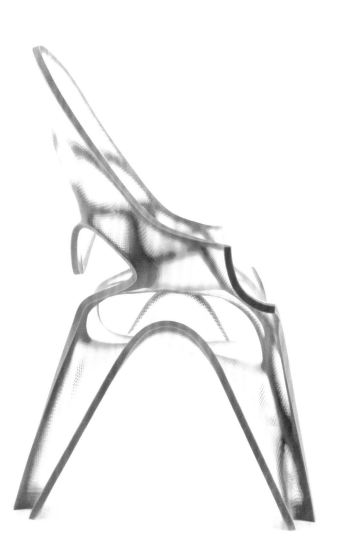

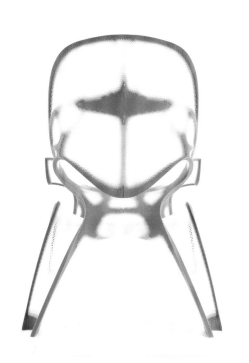

Robert Stuart-Smith

Behavioural Production

Autonomous Swarm-Constructed Architecture

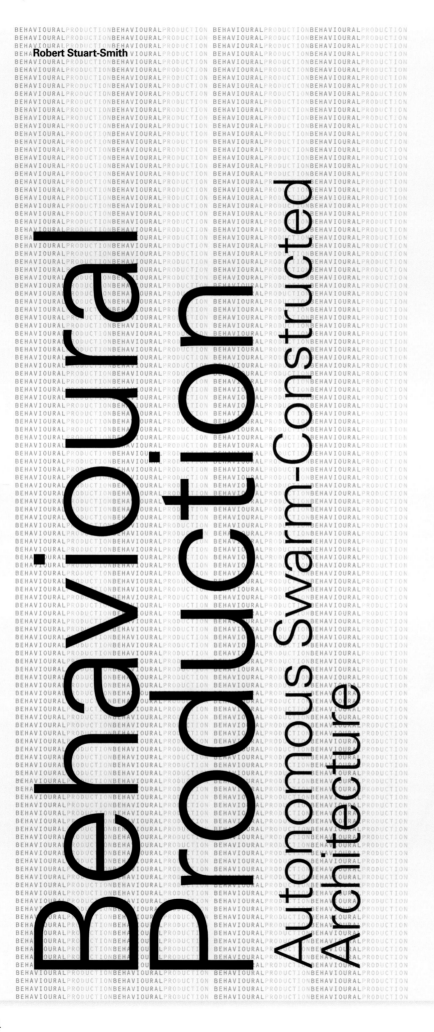

Studio Robert Stuart-Smith/
MinusPlus student team (Ashwin
Balaji, Alejandro García Gadea,
Chiara Leonzio and Martina Rosati),
Looping Matter,
Architectural Association Design
Research Laboratory (AADRL),
London,
2015

An off-board circular-motion wax 3D print deposition strategy. The material contributes significantly to the result.

Until now, parametric processes have largely been confined to the architectural and engineering phases of a building's design. What possibilities, however, do robotics and artificial intelligence programming open up for extending Parametricism's influence into the construction phase? **Robert Stuart-Smith**, a course master at the Architectural Association Design Research Laboratory (AADRL), explores how architecture might adopt autonomous swarm-construction techniques. He describes the research that he has carried out with colleagues and students employing flying multicopters or unmanned aerial vehicles (UAVs) to design and additively manufacture 3D-printed buildings onsite.

Pioneers Alan Turing and John von Neumann foresaw that computers were capable of more than just automated calculation.[1] With artificial intelligence programming now utilised in many industries, will construction also look beyond automation? A number of architectural institutions, particularly the Institute for Computational Design (ICD) at the University of Stuttgart and Gramazio Kohler Research at ETH Zurich, have designed innovative structures that capitalise on the enhanced fabrication capabilities of industrial robots and their ability to be explicitly controlled and automated. 'Behavioural production' investigates how situated robots may augment this research through autonomous participation within design. Sharing Parametricism's interest in encoding architectural and engineering performances as intrinsic properties of design expression, it extends this pursuit to construction. Liberated from adhering to established design styles or methodologies, however, behavioural production enables a potentially more open dialogue between designer, user and the environment. Through real-time engagement and feedback, the non-linear interactions of robots enable creative approaches to construction, and exciting design possibilities.

Aerial Robotic 3D Printing

At the Architectural Association Design Research Laboratory (AADRL) in London, Studio Robert Stuart-Smith (with technical advisors Tyson Hosmer and Manos Matsis, and technical consultants AKT2) has been investigating the design possibilities of a robot swarm-constructed architecture. The research speculates on the use of flying multicopters (UAVs)[2] to additively manufacture (3D print) buildings on-site by layered deposition using bespoke 3D printing hardware attachments. As an automated robotic technology, 3D printing reduces the time, cost, material and waste of construction while enabling design variety and complexity at minimal additional cost. The WinSun Decoration Design Engineering Co has already 3D printed a five-storey apartment building in China,[3] while Dutch company KamerMaker is currently printing an inner-city house in Amsterdan.[4]

These 3D printers deliver economically competitive construction, yet their linear production process and fixed build volume are not ideal for many on-site scenarios. A multicopter swarm-printing system offers increased flexibility and speed through unconstrained three-dimensional movement and parallel production. A 3D print outcome is determined by a combination of flight movements, 3D printer hardware and 3D print material characteristics, necessitating parallel research into all three. The mechanical constraints of multicopter flight and payload provide many challenges to achieving accurate 3D prints. While current prints are not yet suitable for construction, the AADRL studio has developed a number of printing techniques that mitigate a lack of precision in multicopter flight and demonstrate aerial 3D printing is achievable, informing design research into robot flight-control strategies.

Multicopters are already operating on construction sites for tasks such as terrain and construction surveys,[5] but current research suggests further potentials. At ETH Zurich, Gramazio Kohler Research and Raffaello D'Andrea recently assembled a scale-model building composed of lightweight blocks using multicopters.[6] In collaboration with PhD researcher Amar Mirjan they have also demonstrated multicopters wrapping cables and assembling space-frame components.[7] Mirko Kovac, Director of Imperial College's Aerial Robotics Laboratory, has developed a simple multicopter foam 3D printer for repair and emergency scenarios.[8] Large multicopter flight formations are also being performed by Vijay Kumar's research group in the University of Pennsylvania's GRASP Lab. However, while these achievements illustrate substantial technical capabilities, the architectural design potential of aerial robot construction remains relatively unexplored.

Situated Robotics

Multicopters are typically flown manually by remote control or using preprogrammed flight paths. With an additional on-board computer and sensors, a multicopter can be enhanced to become what robotics pioneer and former head of MIT's Artificial Intelligence (AI) Laboratory Rodney Brooks defines as a 'situated robot'.[9] In not requiring a preprogrammed set of instructions, a situated robot can autonomously undertake tasks through programmed responses to locally sensed experiences. Brooks's own work has focused on the development of a 'subsumption architecture',[10] an approach to robotics that allows operational intelligence to emerge from bottom-up rules. Through simple conditional rules, situated robots essentially execute on-board algorithms in the physical world, enabling design-encoded algorithms to form an integral part of an in-situ production process.

Maja Matarić's 20-year-old project Nerd Herd at MIT's AI Lab demonstrated that a decentralised network of situated robots can produce collective behaviours by indirectly cooperating with each other. Through an algorithm encoded with conditional rules, the individivual robots were able to learn and pass on successful behaviours to each other.[11] Ahead of its time, the MIT AI Lab also developed other small distributed robot systems for tasks such as lunar construction, where it was envisaged the robots could shuffle lunar regolith into locations where it might provide environmental shielding around human lunar habitats.[12]

More recently, Radhika Nagpal of Harvard University's Wyss Institute created a robot swarm of 1,024 'kilobots' capable of self-organising

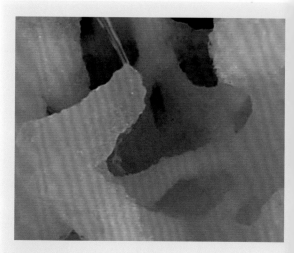

Studio Robert Stuart-Smith/Quadrant student team (Doguscan Aladag, Juan Montiel, Tahel Shaar and Vincent Yeh), Instant Ice, Architectural Association Design Research Laboratory (AADRL), London, 2014

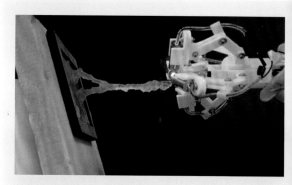

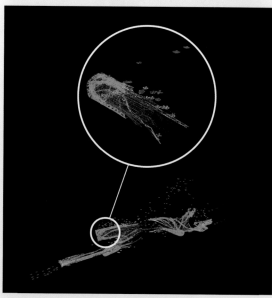

Studio Robert Stuart-Smith/SCL student team (Liu Xiao, Sasila Krishnasreni, Duo Chen and Yiqiang Chen), Swarm Bridge, Architectural Association Design Research Laboratory (AADRL), London, 2014

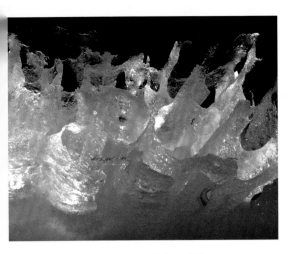

above and opposite: A bespoke ice 3D-printing technique was developed that could be utilised for 3D printing high-resolution porous cavity wall ice constructions.

opposite centre: The bespoke 3D-printing hardware developed for the bridge enables horizontal resin deposition.

opposite bottom: A computer simulation of a 3D printing multicopter swarm constructing the bridge using real-time anticipatory structural analysis.

centre: The pedestrian bridge design is intrinsic to a locally determined construction sequence.

bottom: The bridge design exhibits variations of material density and direction in relation to structural stress and deflection.

into numerous configurations.[13] Computational swarm processes have already been developed by experimental architecture research practice Kokkugia to design architectural projects,[14] while scientists Eric Bonabeau and Guy Theraulaz have demonstrated that termites also construct their habitats through collective behaviours.[15] Utilising stigmergic rules, the construction activities of termites are undertaken in response to the behaviour of other termites, and in relation to their physical environment. This environment is also undergoing constant transformation from the termites' own building activities, resulting in an indirect feedback loop between the termites' actions and perceptions.[16] Similar event-driven rules can govern multicopter 'construction behaviours'. Behavioural production attempts to merge design and production into a singular process that removes distinctions between design creativity and practical construction operations. The benefits of this are twofold: firstly it ensures designers strategise the quantitative impact of their designs on budget, material quantities, construction logistics and time; and secondly it expands design possibilities by engaging with realisation variables as potential contributors to final design outcomes.

Autonomous On-site Construction

Although 3D printing multicopters could construct predetermined designs, the AADRL research engages in varied degrees of autonomous real-time design on-site with the goal of constructing spaces that could not easily be realised by other means. This is undertaken within speculative design scenarios involving the development of bespoke computer simulations that aim to generate qualitative design effects intrinsic to an on-site production process.

For example, student team Quadrant's project Instant Ice (2014) speculated that multicopters are able to operate in climates that humans find difficult or dangerous to work in. The project proposed utilising multicopters to undertake 3D-printed ice constructions for the building and maintaining of shelters in remote polar regions. It was envisaged that aerial robots could sensitively monitor the dynamically changing properties of ice and continuously reinforce areas where the construction had started to meld by 3D printing additional ice. Multicopters could also harvest ice from locally available snow, demonstrating a closed-loop material cycle. The research developed ice cavity wall constructions with high thermal performance through algorithmically controlled flight simulations. Printing activities adjusted to the changing material properties of ice in fluctuating temperatures. The research demonstrated ice 3D prints and flight simulations separately, yet successfully embraced temporal aspects of ice construction within a design strategy that was inseparable from a simulated construction process.

The construction of bridges in remote locations with limited access or infrastructure was also explored by student team SCL. The Swarm Bridge (2014) project sought to construct a bridge incrementally from two opposing sides, which could then be joined in the middle to create a unified structure. This strategy involves a change in structural type during construction, converting two independent cantilevers into a single-span beam. Both conditions distribute stress and deflection differently, requiring different optimal organisations of material. SCL proposed 3D printing a bridge between two cliffs using lightweight fibre-composite construction while sensitively responding to this change in structural type. Recognising that deviations from the original design model might occur throughout the construction process due to wind, real-time anticipatory structural analysis was introduced. This enabled multicopters to spontaneously stop current activities and build additional structural supports when required to maintain the structural integrity of the bridge. The project successfully mixed explicit predesigned 3D form with real-time structural analysis and feedback to construct a structurally optimised bridge that emerged from the simulated local interaction of robot constructors, the environment and already 3D-printed material.

While SCL's research developed resin 3D-printing hardware and construction simulations, student team Void employed multicopters to work as an actual construction swarm. Rather than 3D printing, in The Thread (2014) Void delivered a tensile-structure installation composed of lightweight nylon thread. Multicopters undertook aerial weaving and bundling operations that are theoretically scaleable and able to be used to construct larger structures. The swarm performed in an autonomous and choreographed manner, achieving a three-dimensional weave of threads only repeatable if constructed with the same specific flight sequence.

While Void's project involved multicopter flight movements that were generated in computer simulations, students AerialFloss have demonstrated multicopters utilising situated decision-making to undertake autonomous thread wrapping, and avoidance of already wrapped threads. An installation similar to Void's could therefore be constructed from the execution of an algorithm onboard each multicopter (rather than off-board as Void achieved). The algorithm could run in parallel on a team of multicopters simultaneously and embody bottom-up rules that allow each multicopter to respond to real-time computer vision, enabling construction activities to be adapted to suit different physical sites. This process is non-linear and subject to scientist Edward Lorenz's term 'sensitive dependance',[17] where small differences in a site's initial spatial configuration could result in extremely different design outcomes from the exact same algorithm being implemented.

The robustness of a design algorithm must therefore be evaluated by the usefulness and design interest of resulting constructions across many different sites. A design emerges from the robot swarm's spatial and social negotiations on-site. As a stigmergic process, design input operates at the level of an algorithm, or through on-site activities that change the physical environment that the robots respond to. AerialFloss has also developed protocols that determine robot actions in relation to their perception of camera-vision markers, colours, people and objects. Human participation in design is therefore possible via 3D design models and the coding of on-board algorithms defined prior to construction, and also through the placement of physical markers throughout construction, allowing human observers to indirectly constrain and augment robotic construction. This recasts the architectural possibilities of robotic construction into a potentially more open dialogue between designer, user and the environment.

Although in its infancy, situated robotics is progressing rapidly and extending human capabilities into unknown territories. With this, new design and construction possibilities are emerging that warrant further speculation and development. While remote or hazardous environments provide obvious applications for autonomous construction, conventional sites also offer exciting opportunities.

Studio Robert Stuart-Smith/ Void student team (Karthikeyan Arunachalam, Maria García, Alejandra Rojas and Mel Sfeir), The Thread, Architectural Association Design Research Laboratory (AADRL), London, 2014

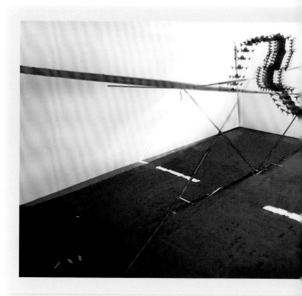

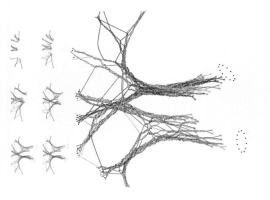

above: A computer simulation generates the design and determines the flight movements required for its construction.

opposite: A 3D tensile installation created by multicopter autonomous flight.

below: Three multicopters undertake the cooperative building of the tensile installation through autonomous choreographic movement.

Studio Robert Stuart-Smith, AerialFloss student team (Patchara Ruentongdee, Kai-Jui Tsao and Zhang Qiao), ArialFloss, Architectural Association Design Research Laboratory (AADRL), London, 2015

A multicopter autonomously navigates through a field of threads while avoiding collisions.

Sensor technologies are expanding our ability to identify and locate the spatial, geological and chemical composition of the environment; for example, Consumer Physics's SCiO portable spectrometers can determine the chemical composition of objects, while LiDAR (Light Detection and Ranging) now delivers exceptional detail for 3D scan surveys.

Conventional construction is unable to address this detailed site information, however situated robot design and construction could enable buildings to match or go beyond the compositional matrix of each individual site in sensitive and profound ways. Behavioural production suggests an alternative approach to architectural design that is capable of extending design influence into the seemingly pragmatic domain of construction. This can be achieved by engaging directly with situated robots that can operate autonomously, collectively, and in relation to people and the environment throughout a construction process. As demonstrated by the AADRL speculative work described here, this shifts design into new roles that are able to operate alongside, or replace, existing methods, and potentially resituates the designer as the encoder of autonomous robotic behaviours for the construction of architectures still unknown. ◬

Notes
1. Alan M Turing, 'Computing Machinery And Intelligence', *Mind*, 49, 1950. Pp 433–60.
2. 'What Is a MultiCopter and How Does it Work?': http://copter.ardupilot.com/wiki/introduction/what-is-a-multicopter-and-how-does-it-work/.
3. Rory Stott, 'Chinese Company Constructs the World's Tallest 3D Printed Building', *ArchDaily*, 26 January 2015: www.archdaily.com/591331/chinese-company-creates-the-world-s-tallest-3d-printed-building/.
4. Toby Sterling, 'Amsterdam Canal House Built with 3-D Printer', 14 March 2014: www.phys.org/news/2014-03-amsterdam-canal-house-built-d.html.
5. Remote Aerial Surveys (RAS), 'UAVs Helping Construction from Start to Finish': www.remoteaerialsurveys.co.uk/article/uavs-helping-construction-from-start-to-finish/12.
6. Fabio Gramazio, Matthias Kohler and Jan Willmann (eds), *The Robot Touch: How Robots Change Architecture*, Park Books (Zurich), 2014.
7. *Ibid*, pp 310–23.
8. G Hunt *et al*, '3D Printing with Flying Robots', *IEEE International Conference on Robotics and Automation (ICRA)*, Hong Kong, May 2014, pp 4493–9.
9. Rodney Allen Brooks, *Flesh and Machines: How Robots Will Change Us*, Pantheon (New York), 2002, p 51.
10. *Ibid*, p 41.
11. Jerry Shine, 'Herd Mentality', *Wired*, 4.06: http://archive.wired.com/wired/archive/4.06/esherd_pr.html.
12. Brooks, *op cit*, p 55.
13. 'A Self-Organizing Thousand-Robot Swarm', Wyss Institute, 14 August 2014: http://wyss.harvard.edu/viewpressrelease/164.
14. Roland Snooks and Robert Stuart-Smith, 'Non Linear Formation: Or How to Resist the Parametric Subversion of Computational Design', in Pavlos Xanthropoulos and Ioulietta Zindrou (eds), *Apomechanes*, Asprimera Publications (Athens), 2010, pp 140–7.
15. Scott Camazine *et al*, 'Termite Mound Building', in Scott Camazine, *Self-Organization in Biological Systems*, Princeton University Press (New Jersey), 2001, p 377.
16. *Ibid*.
17. Edward N Lorenz, *The Essence of Chaos*, University of Washington Press (Seattle, WA), 1993, p 167.

Marc Fornes

The Art of the Prototypical

Poised between design research and full-scale realisation, prototypes in architecture provide a significant stepping stone for innovation. Through his New York-based studio THEVERYMANY, **Mark Fornes** explores the possibilities of coding and computer prototcols for design and fabrication through art installations and architectural structures. As prototypical projects, they are each defined by a single architectural concern, like a structure, enclosure or porosity; the intention being to realise the structure as a pleasurable spatial experience with potential for scalability.

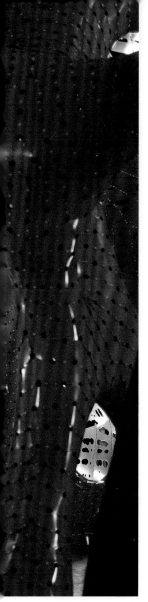

The work of MARC FORNES/THEVERYMANY may be described as 'prototypical architectures', in which 'prototypical' – an adjective – extends a logical suite that begins with the sample (a test of a precise element within a unit), building to the prototype (a unit or relationship between units) and from there up to the mock-up (a number of units set up and not assembled completely).

The premise of each project is based on precisely defined architectural concerns, such as structure, enclosure, porosity etc. Through a process of empirical and serial experiments in both computational descriptive geometry and material systems, development grows from the scale of a unit, to a system of units, to an entire project, where all of its nature is fully tested at 1:1 scale – including, most importantly, the pleasure of its spatial experience – with the potential for further scalability.

This article outlines the driving parameters behind THEVERYMANY's prototypical architectures, including the unique terminologies that have matured in tandem with the development process itself.

EXPLICIT AND ENCODED PROTOCOLS

One of the initial premises within the work of THEVERYMANY is related to the specificity of the process: all morphologies result from explicit protocols – or finite series of steps, unambiguous instructions, hierarchically organised into a linear sequence, and translated through the shortest possible notation into an operational algorithm.

The creation of a design process by applied logic in hierarchical steps is not unique to computer science (it can be analogue), unless its logic is explicitly encoded to be interpreted by computers. THEVERYMANY's protocols are explicitly written within a text file, articulated within a computational syntax (Python), call upon a vocabulary or methods from external libraries (Rhinocommon) and are finally executed within a software environment (Rhino3D).

PROTOCOL OF PRECISE INDETERMINATION

Such protocols are defined and driven through numerically controlled parameters, and therefore are precise. There is no such thing as a computational 'maybe'! Yet also and most of all the protocol is considered precise because it calls least upon randomness: one wants to be able to run the same code twice and get the same result each time if one wants to implement or debug a specific code or geometrical problem, especially if a special or uncommon case.

While the operational logic requires precision in order to be implementable, especially when fabrication is involved, there is also a request from a design standpoint to leave room for an element of surprise for the purpose of exploration and invention. Yet even if the protocol is the sum of very deterministic steps (assuming the author wrote every line of code, and understands the method's logic and limitations / black box) it is still often required to execute the code in order to visualise its result. Due to the number of lines, steps and conditions ('if ... then ...' statements), it is impossible for the author to anticipate the result exactly, and therefore writing computational protocols of design constantly includes a factor of indetermination: one likes a moment of the result and yet it isn't obvious at first sight to its author what has triggered such a result – the happy mistake, to be understood, controlled, designed upon and finally implemented. The amount of surprise or distortion between the anticipated and actual results could be defined as 'inertia of the protocol' or 'resonance within the system' – results even higher than expected – but not to be confused with the field of Emergence Theory that would require a much more exhaustive and sophisticated set of criteria.

FROM FORM FINDING TO STRUCTURANT MORPHOLOGIES

Based on a history of empirical serial testings focusing on the translation of digital geometries to physical reassemblies, the work of THEVERYMANY was forced to address degrees of failures – from the most dramatic failures such as total collapse, to invisible logistical issues detrimental to the possibility of scalability. Since at first exclusively empirical, this sharpened an understanding of structure and focused interest onto performant self-supportive structures, such as hyper-thin shell structures. At the level of the low-funded installation, the integration of the different into a single system is also cost-efficient for its reduction of complexity (number of elements, assembly types etc).

INTENSIVE CURVATURE VS EXTENSIVE CURVATURE

The performance of hyper-thin self-supported structures is achieved through extensive curvature – a principle based on maximising the overall double curvature of a surface or volume in order to take advantage of its structural capacities. Yet double curvature in itself is not enough. While the work of Frei Otto demonstrates that the structural model of the soap bubble is far more performant than that of a box, such a model is relatively less performant

MARC FORNES/
THEVERYMANY,
Louis Vuitton
Pop-Up Shop,
Selfridges,
London,
2012

Technology and material
innovation contribute to the
evolution of the research
of the studio. The pop-up
shop for Louis Vuitton
demonstrated the largest-
scale application to date of
carbon fibre.

MARC FORNES/
THEVERYMANY,
Double Agent White,
Atelier Calder,
Sache,
France,
2012

The performance of hyper-thin
self-supported structures is
achieved through extensive
curvature – a principle based
on maximising the overall
double curvature of a surface
or volume in order to take
advantage of its structural
capacities.

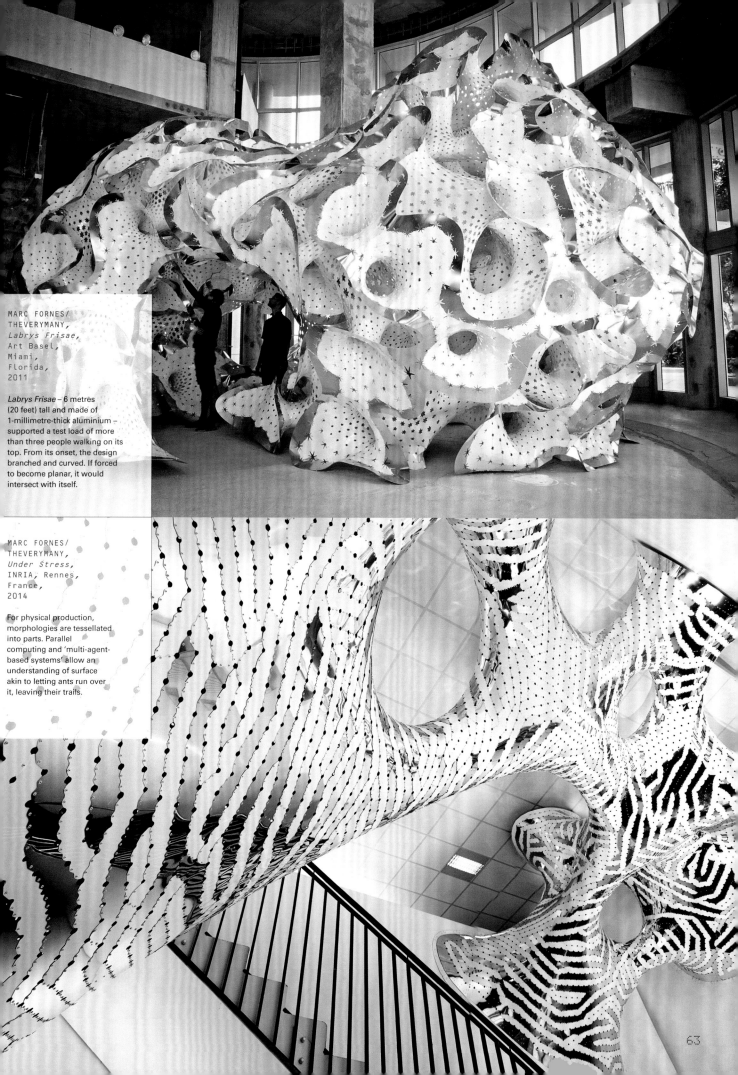

MARC FORNES/
THEVERYMANY,
Labrys Frisae,
Art Basel,
Miami,
Florida,
2011

Labrys Frisae – 6 metres (20 feet) tall and made of 1-millimetre-thick aluminium – supported a test load of more than three people walking on its top. From its onset, the design branched and curved. If forced to become planar, it would intersect with itself.

MARC FORNES/
THEVERYMANY,
Under Stress,
INRIA, Rennes,
France,
2014

For physical production, morphologies are tessellated into parts. Parallel computing and 'multi-agent-based systems' allow an understanding of surface akin to letting ants run over it, leaving their trails.

if scaled to the size of a building. Scale matters: what is perceived as double curved at an architectural scale can often be approximated as the compound of straight lines or planes, and therefore has to be compensated by either material thickness or, in the case of active tension, heavy masts able to sustain the tension forces, such as in Otto's Munich stadium (1972).

Intensive curvature intends to maximise double curvature everywhere (extensive) yet constrain maximum radii of curvature. Morphologies based on intensive curvature tend to curl in all directions (in order to maximise the differentiation of radii, but also the direction of curvature) and compound 'closed-profile' elements, such as thick lattice networks (as having a tight radius in one direction at least, and therefore extremely structurally performant).

BASE MESH VS BASIC MESH

Morphologies such as those within Frei Otto's work can be digitally simulated from a 'simpler' planar mesh with a series of anchors locked in place (vertices, curves etc) and the application of forces. Even though it acts as an abstract elastic fabric during the simulation process, such a starting mesh can exist in planar form without topological issues such as overlaps or self-intersections.

The work of THEVERYMANY is based on a two-step process, emphasising further development into the creation of the initial base mesh topology as well as into the relaxation process itself. Meshes are vertices (coordinates), edges (relationships) and faces (representation) with directions, that can potentially represent endless types of complex and non-linear morphologies: compounds of open/closed, non-manifolds, branching or recombination, etc. As such they can most often not exist in planar form and require for example to be built through multiple additive or difference Boolean operations in three-dimensional space.

Prototypical structures such as THEVERYMANY's Labrys Frisae (2011) – a 10-by-10-metre (33-by-33-foot) structure, 6 metres (20 feet) tall and built from aluminium sheets that are less than a millimetre thick – could nonetheless support its dead load, as well as the live loads of multiple people climbing to its top. This loading test has been empirically tested with up to three people freely and simultaneously ascending it.

THEVERYMANY

The work of THEVERYMANY has been exploring the physical production of structural morphologies through the development of custom protocols of tessellation (the description of the surface/mesh through simple elements, from triangles/quads to irregular polygons). The issue demonstrated through serial physical prototyping of such systems is that they rely on singularity: each face (triangle/quad/polygon of *n* number of edges) is materialised as a panel, making the total number of elements and unique parts potentially endless. While this situation may be great for the design of patterns (directionality, intensities etc), it presents a nightmare to physically reassemble. The creation of parts becomes, on one hand, simpler because they are not curved (and therefore do not require moulding/carving/printing), yet complexity re-emerges through logistics: naming conventions, production, double-checks, and the increased risk of error and long amounts of time in reassembly.

FROM THE VERY MANY TO THE VERY LEAST

For protocols addressing such logistical issues of reassembly, the issue becomes one of turning the very many into the very least number of parts. THEVERYMANY's initial direction was based on a principle of recombination: tessellation of surface/meshes according to selected criteria (for example, smaller elements at tightest curvature) recombined into larger sets – such as stripes – rather than accepting the sum of singularities as material system.

The very first example – invented for THEVERYMANY's *n|Strip* project (2010) – was based on a linear recombination of singular panels as chains, or striped morphologies, where the sum of singular planar parts are potentially developable as well (if no issues such as self-intersection exist) and therefore transformed as a material system. This dramatically reduced the number of parts while, as a by-product, dramatically increasing structural performance by increasing redundancies of connections to multiple neighbours.

FROM DESCRIPTIVE GEOMETRY TO SEARCH PROTOCOLS

The issue with material systems of linear stripes created through recombination is that while such protocols allow local choices for best-fit behaviour (according to, for instance, curvature) within each stripe, there is no overall knowledge of the entire system.

The introduction of parallel computing and 'multi-agent-based systems' allows agents – or encapsulated sets of rules – to understand others at each loop, and exchange feedback. This means picking seeds, for instance at the

MARC FORNES/ THEVERYMANY, *y/Struc/Surf*, Centre Pompidou, Paris, 2011

y/Struc/Surf at the Pompidou is an early example of a linear recombination of singular panels as chains, creating 'structural stripes', which have become a primary research premise of THEVERYMANY. The recombination of panels into stripes reduces the number of parts for assembly while also augmenting structural properties.

The work of THEVERYMANY has been exploring the physical production of structural morphologies through the development of custom protocols of tessellation

The results are fully
immersive experiences
to visit, engage, play
in and lose oneself in.

edges, and running them like ants onto the morphology, leaving a trail. When the trail is too long, they die and the path becomes material stripes.

The invention of such local reading to describe a mesh and define a linear material system allows for non-mathematicians/computer scientists to bypass primitive laws of traditional descriptive geometry and replace it by a numerous 'population' of agents crawling onto the morphology. From there, the author can decide through test trial errors the best path of progress according to the reading of local conditions.

COMPETITIVE RULE SETS AND SCHIZOPHRENIC BEHAVIOURS

However, descriptive systems based on search can often not rely on one single set of rules. Due to the nature and complexity required by structurant morphologies based on intensive curvature, a rule that solves a problem for one local condition often triggers new problems elsewhere. Such protocol of description requires competitive rule sets in order to find the best set of rules, and the best-fit parameters to solve overall the maximum amount of conditions through local decision making. The behaviours of stripes observed with such rules are nervous, fighting one another, and therefore referred to as 'schizophrenic'.

Protocols – such as for THEVERYMANY's *y/Struc/Surf* project (2011) for the Centre Pompidou in Paris – feed their agents with the local parameters in reverse order of best fit; the solution that first passes the test isn't necessarily the best, but rather the first one acceptable, triggering a best average solution.

FROM NON-LINEAR MORPHOLOGIES TO SETS OF LINEAR DESCRIPTIONS

The trails of such agents, once converted to geometries (with attributes such as relative width, thickness, technicalities and other detailing), can be digitally cut as linear stripes within sheet material. Typical fitness criteria for production are length and shape. If too long, stripes can't fit on standard sheets of material or a specific machine bed. If too curly, stripes won't nest or layer well for packaging; yet if too straight or similar in shape, it becomes harder to differentiate them during physical reassembly. Also, if the stripes are too long, they won't work well at physical high differentiation of curvature such as recombinatory or splitting nodes; though if too short, the process is back at square one (singularities), with too many parts.

COLORATION VS COLOUR(S)

Colours are obviously highly subjective, submitting to trends and fashions. Choosing a colour, and moreover standing for it for years, can take its toll for an architect. Computation and procedural protocols of tessellation have opened up new paradigms: each physical part can be assigned an attribute of a single colour, therefore the sum of the parts can precisely approximate gradients (rather than the fuzziness of earlier airbrush solutions).

Coloration defines the procedural art of applying multiple colours across sets of parts. For example, gradients can be parametrised smooth (depending on the number of parts), stepped with precise amplitude (contrast from one part to the other), linear (in the blend from one colour to another), non-linear (with local intensities), with two or multiple colours, zebras with a single constant colour, or mixed with other gradients through precise modulo alternation. The possibilities are endless. The effect of such coloration protocols can become extremely intricate, therefore potentially less subjective to initial prejudice about specific single colours, since the complex logics established have first to be analysed and understood (both at global and local scale) before even getting one's mind around it.

PROTOTYPICAL ARCHITECTURES VS ARCHITECTURE

From a research standpoint, the work of THEVERYMANY has focused on the invention of the algorithmic descriptive of mesh geometry via planar stripes and their physical reassembly into self-supported doubly curved surfaces without the need for expensive moulds or temporary scaffolding. The results are fully immersive experiences to visit, engage, play in and lose oneself in. Even though these structures are often temporary interior 'installations' funded through art, there is a focused motivation to become permanent, to grow up in scale, and to be exposed to more elements, live loads, multiple programmes and very different cultures and contexts. The aim is not to be exclusively known as prototypical architectures among the expert audience of a specialised field, but rather to operate fundamentally as architecture. △

MARC FORNES/THEVERYMANY, *Vaulted Willow*, Edmonton, Alberta, Canada, 2014

above: Computation has opened up the road of gradient coloration – linear (or non-linear) blending of one colour to another, or furthermore for multiple zebras, where each of the two colours can be their own gradient. The analytical rereading of geometry provides the opportunity not to force colours onto a morphology, but to enhance its variation by colouring different surfaces, ends and zones of curvature.

left: Because the amount of tessellated parts is potentially endless – a logistical nightmare – they must be recombined according to best-fitness criteria. One criterion to consider for recombination is the way parts nest on a sheet of the material from which they will be digitally cut.

The Block Research Group (BRG) at the Institute of Technology in Architecture, ETH Zurich, led by Philippe Block and Tom Van Mele, focuses on research in equilibrium analysis, computational form-finding and the fabrication of curved-surface structures. Here, **Philippe Block** describes how

Philippe Block

PARAMET
STRUCTU
CONGENI

Parametricism's preoccupation with expressive surface structures enables architecture 'to learn from the past' and draw on the rich seam of historical knowledge that has informed the complex curved structures of the Gothic cathedral builders and modern masters.

RICISM'S

RAL

ALITY

The design and construction of shell structures is an inherently historical field, the greatest examples having been realised in the past. These reach back to the Gothic era, with its sensational stone cathedrals, to the tile vaulting of Rafael Guastavino at the turn of the 20th century, and more recently to the period of the great shell builders of the 1950s and 1960s led by the likes of Eduardo Torroja, Félix Candela and Heinz Isler in reinforced concrete, or Eladio Dieste in reinforced brick. It is only now, however, that this knowledge is being reintroduced and enhanced through new research.

Thanks to recent innovations in structural engineering, particularly in the development of extremely flexible and fast structurally informed computational design methods, as well as in multi-criteria optimisation techniques, the gap between structural and architectural complex curved geometry is narrowing. The potential of this newly generated knowledge is that it allows for truly holistic designs that find a balance between form and force. The terms 'expressive' and 'structurally efficient' are no longer oxymoronic, but can be synonymous. Parametricism proposes a style that capitalises on expressive surface structures, allowing geometry in architecture to adequately address the complex, dynamic and programmatic requirements of contemporary institutions.

Block Research Group (BRG), Funicular funnel shell, ETH Zurich, 2013

previous spread and above: Controlling the flow of forces through explicit form and force diagrams, the new graphical form-finding approaches developed by the BRG allow the careful shaping of expressive and structurally efficient shells. This shell acts in compression on the inside, balanced by a tension ring along the cantilevering perimeter.

LEARNING FROM THE PAST: THE DECLINE AND CHALLENGES OF SHELLS

The use of continuous shell structures in architecture and the knowledge required for their design and construction declined significantly from the 1960s for a number of reasons. Firstly, they are difficult to integrate into programmatic needs, particularly in multilevel buildings, and they present a variety of issues in the arena of building physics, as well as challenges in architectural detailing. Formally they fell out of fashion, especially during the rise of 20th-century Modernism. Given the typical costs involved in the construction of formwork, they are materially and labour intensive, and ultimately the available types of optimised geometry for shell structures have until recently been limited.

Despite these many challenges, however, the use of shell structures can also offer opportunities, as will be argued here. By proposing a style that is dominated by expressive surface structures, Parametricism can utilise complex geometry to address the multifarious demands of contemporary architecture, for example by providing more intuitive and natural ways to navigate space using the inherent semiological potentials of shapes. It thus addresses one of the above-mentioned key reasons why shell structures have fallen into disuse: the challenge of integrating programmatic needs in an elegant manner.

In no small way, this reason for the declining use of shell structures may be attributed to issues of building physics; for example, how to avoid thermal bridges,

how to integrate insulation without covering a shell's surface, or how to interface with vertical walls or in between floors. The inherent flatness of floors is at odds with the continuous curves of a shell structure. An astonishing structure like Félix Candela's posthumous Oceanogràfic in Valencia, an oceanarium representing various marine habitats that was completed in 2003, arguably loses its eloquence – visible only during its construction phase – right after the formwork has been taken out; once that raw construction is filled with walls, facades, building systems, lighting and so on, it becomes a less compelling form. How might shells be designed so they are also floors, or how can floors become shells? Finding a language – and an efficient and cost-effective means of construction – that integrates shells beyond their occasional appearance as singular building roofs or pavilion structures offers great potential to return meaning and purposefulness to these elegant structural systems.

BUILDING AT ANY 'COST'

Complex architectural geometry typically comes at the expense of structural elegance and construction efficiency. Shell structures can address the former with varying degrees of success, but they all too quickly become unconvincing if they do not also address the latter; that is, if they cannot be constructed in an efficient or generally appropriate manner that considers the important role of local, cultural, and (socio-) economic factors. Shells typically require full and rigid formworks. Furthermore, the materials used to build formwork

Félix Candela, Oceanogràfic, Valencia, Spain, 2003

top: After Candela's death in 1997, engineers Carlos Lázaro and Alberto Domingo of CMD Ingenieros continued this oceanarium project, realising the shell as a thin sheet of only 6 centimetres (2 inches) in steel-fibre concrete spanning 40 metres (130 feet).

designtoproduction, Destroyed formwork of SANAA's Rolex Learning Center, Ecole Polytechnique Fédérale de Lausanne (EPFL), Switzerland, 2009

above: The custom CNC-cut shuttering of the optimised/ simplified formwork of the university study centre's concrete shell reduced to a pile of non-reusable waste.

shuttering are often used only once, as they are customised for a specific, doubly curved geometry. For example, Fabian Scheurer of designtoproduction has wistfully described the formwork for the construction of SANAA's Rolex Learning Center at the Ecole Polytechnique Fédérale de Lausanne (EPFL) in Switzerland (2009) as his first large-scale timber structure, though it only stood for a few months.[1]

Structures such as Scheurer's for the EPFL study centre are therefore frequently not competitive in a profit-driven market, particularly where labour is expensive. Although some freeform concrete shells have been realised in recent years, these contemporary examples are usually signature buildings, where budget, materials or other constraints are not necessarily a central concern. Though these structures serve their place, a wider variety of applications in more diverse contexts is possible.

DISCOVERING OPPORTUNITIES

Advances in computer graphics, and especially the rapidly expanding possibilities enabled by computer modelling and generation techniques have resulted in an explosion of formal explorations in architectural design. New and complex shapes can be generated regardless of their structural stability or feasibility. The structural solutions required to build these new shapes often use an 'awkward accumulation of materials' rather than 'resistance through form' as Eladio Dieste termed it.[2] This leads to an approach to building that is intellectually – and often also architecturally – unsatisfactory. For example, a lack

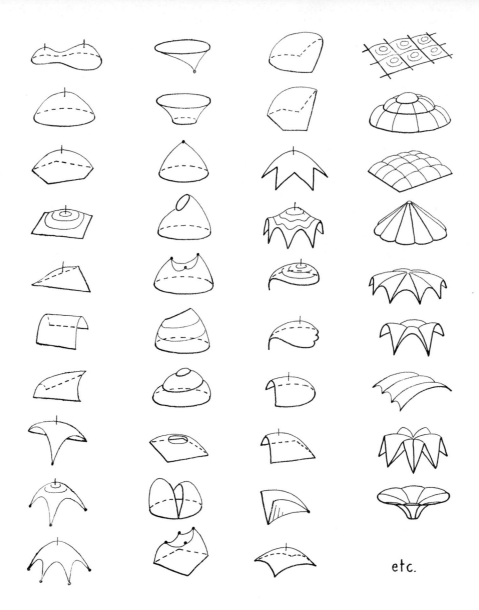

etc.

Heinz Isler, 'New Shapes for Shells', 1959

left: At the First Congress of the International Association for Shell Structures (IASS) in Madrid in 1959, Isler presented his paper 'New Shapes for Shells', which included an illustration of 39 playful sketched shapes for shells, with 'etc.' suggesting infinite variations.

of structural thinking during the design process leads to constructions such as Frank Gehry's Walt Disney Concert Hall in Los Angeles (2003), where the structural engineers come in later to bring the architect's imaginative sketches into three dimensions. Such a unidirectional process results in heavy structures, wasted materials and inelegant details.

Arguably, architecture has failed if it is merely a freeform skin with a substructure, like the flat building fronts propped up from behind on the set of a Western, where it is only an image lacking materiality. Concrete shell structures, if properly designed and constructed in a process involving both architects and engineers, are able to cover large spaces at minimal material cost through efficient compressive and/or tensile membrane stresses, becoming fully three-dimensional functional forms rather than just screens. Shell shapes now go beyond the optimised ideal shapes and typologies developed by engineers and mathematicians in the heydays of shells in the 1950s and 1960s. They are fluid in their potential, which is made possible by

new design approaches and tools. However, history can teach us much more. Structural concepts from the past can become driving forces in contemporary design; for example, traditional rib patterns can drive an aesthetic. More importantly, new efficiencies in fabrication and construction inspired by forgotten or lost knowledge can bring the entire methodology full circle. Parametricism needs real structural and engineering innovations to differentiate itself from purely image-driven architecture and to realise the full potential of complex curved geometry.

Tracing the vagaries of the use or disuse of shell structures is not simply a matter of following changes in stylistic taste or fashion. Learning from the past helps us to build in the present with logic and restraint. Digital and technological innovations and advances now allow us to achieve complex and spectacular geometries almost regardless of material or financial cost. However, the planet's decreasing resources, and widening awareness and public opinion regarding the use of materials or size of carbon footprints demand that architects

Block Research Group
(BRG) with Escobedo
Construction,
Prototype of cable-
net and fabric-
formed thin shell,
Buda, Texas, 2015

This thin-shell prototype was
formed using a lightweight,
prestressed cable-net and
fabric formwork using
mainly standard shoring and
scaffolding elements.

engage with these issues. Complexity for the sake of complexity, especially if accompanied by a disregard for material flows or financial resources, is not intrinsically interesting or stimulating. We need to be asking the question: can we do the same – or more – with less?

REIMAGINING THE TRADITIONAL

Parametricism favours complex geometry and curved surface structures and therefore demands a continued push towards increased research and innovation in shell structures. Additionally, it justifies the value of shells that can be more efficiently constructed through (pre-)fabrication or other methods to avoid material waste or to better integrate building technologies. In several ongoing projects, the Block Research Group (BRG) at ETH Zurich is developing novel design approaches for shells as well as exploring new construction methods and logics to create these expressive, resource-efficient structural forms. The work shows that structural engineering can go beyond making a given geometry produce true innovation, and that designing with constraints need not constrain progress.

Heinz Isler may have been teasing in 1959 when, in his illustration of 39 playful sketched shapes for shells, he simply included the abbreviation 'etc.' in the final space, leaving the door open for infinite variations,[3] but we now have the tools to realise his vision. Morphing from one shape to the next, we have a wide vocabulary of fully flexible possibilities at our disposal. Nevertheless, the appropriate use of materials or other, more locally distinct limitations must remain central to the design and construction of shells.

For the Fábrica de Cultura, an arts school in Barranquilla, Colombia, by Urban-Think Tank with the BRG and the Chair of Architecture and Building Systems, ETH Zurich (planned to enter the construction phase in 2016), the BRG designed a tile-vaulted shell for the auditorium within a number of strict specifications. The compression-only shell needed to span a space of 20 by 40 metres (65 x 130 feet) and be optimised for construction using local labour and materials. As well as being expressive, it also needed to meet the high room-acoustical standards necessary for a performance space – all within light budget limits. The project took full advantage of the 'thrust network

analysis' approach, which is a three-dimensional extension of graphic statics.[4] Thanks to the explicit control of the relation between the form and forces of the shell through geometrically connected diagrams, these multiple criteria could be satisfied simultaneously during the design process. The geometrically dependent form and force diagrams functioned as parametric models, constrained to generate exclusively compression-only solutions.

Tile vaults are unreinforced masonry structures made of bricks and fast-setting mortar. The technique allows for the construction of complex shell structures without the need for formwork, making them inherently more economic and less wasteful in terms of materials and labour. The tile vault of the auditorium in Barranquilla will be a self-supporting permanent formwork for the concrete shell, picking up dead load and reducing costs – of the formwork itself, but also of the foundations that would otherwise be needed to support it. This has the additional benefit that while the concrete cures for the required 28 days, construction and finishing will continue beneath the shell, further optimising building processes, time and costs. Reinterpreting traditional construction techniques within a set of locally defined constraints thus reveals that new, economically and materially optimised shell structures are feasible in a surprising context.

By foregoing the need for disposable formworks which are destroyed once construction is complete, and instead making the formwork a permanent and expressive part of the structure, the tile vault reduces

waste from construction. Similarly, approaches that externalise supports or require minimal or no foundations represent efficient use of materials. Lightweight, flexible formwork systems can also reduce the amount of material needed, especially for the falsework. Shuttering can be replaced by fabric, and falsework such as scaffolding can be replaced by cables or rods supported by an external frame at its boundaries. The formwork system offers a degree of control over the shape so that it can be easily optimised for improved structural behaviour and other criteria. Expensive, unique or customised parts are reduced to the minimum.

SUPERCHARGING SHELLS

Another area of potential for reduction is of course energy use. The NEST-HiLo research and innovation unit in Dübendorf, Switzerland, seeks to address many challenges related to the use of shell structures, including most prominently the issue of energy consumption and production, as well as the drastic reduction of required materials. Designed by the BRG and Chair of Architecture and Building Systems (ETH Zurich) with supermanoeuvre and Zwarts & Jansma Architects, the project (due to be completed in 2016) is more than just a shell with the singular function of simply spanning or covering, and is instead at once a structure, facade, insulation, a heating and cooling system, and a generator of energy.

The roof system is designed as a lightweight, doubly curved, thin sandwich shell structure, its shape structurally optimised to push the limits of what is

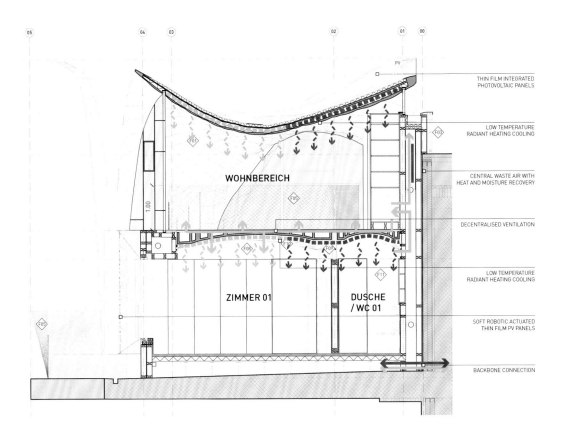

WOHNBEREICH

ZIMMER 01

DUSCHE / WC 01

PV

THIN FILM INTEGRATED
PHOTOVOLTAIC PANELS

LOW TEMPERATURE
RADIANT HEATING COOLING

CENTRAL WASTE AIR WITH
HEAT AND MOISTURE RECOVERY

DECENTRALISED VENTILATION

LOW TEMPERATURE
RADIANT HEATING COOLING

SOFT ROBOTIC ACTUATED
THIN FILM PV PANELS

BACKBONE CONNECTION

possible in concrete. Its thinness and large surface area function like a radiator for heat transfer into the space within using a hydronic, low-temperature heating and cooling system. Polyurethane foam insulation will be used to achieve a low thermal transmittance at a small thickness. On top, optimally distributed, high-efficiency thin-film photovoltaic cells will be used for solar energy generation. To minimise thermal bridging, the connection between the glass facade and the shell demands the sandwich design, increasing the structural depth and reducing sensitivity to external loads and imperfections.

The floor design of the HiLo unit represents the most dramatic material savings within the NEST project. Its structure consists of a thin funicular vault made of concrete, stiffened by a system of fins on its extrados, and supported by the unit's primary frame structure at its four corners. These corners are connected by tension ties to absorb the horizontal thrusts of the funicular shell. This solution is inspired by built examples in tile vaulting in which thin vaults are stiffened by diaphragms, also called spandrel walls. The structural system is designed in cast concrete to achieve a thickness of only 2 centimetres (0.8 inches) for both vault and fins. Introducing funicular vaulting results in an extremely lightweight floor system with savings of more than 70 per cent in terms of both material and weight compared to prestressed, hollow-core slabs which are already considered to be optimal.

top: The HiLo shell functions as a radiator using a hydronic, low-temperature heating and cooling system and has high-efficiency thin-film photovoltaic cells applied on top. A structural sandwich shell with polyurethane foam insulation as its core solves the potential thermal bridge along the line of the glass facade, resulting in a continuous lower surface of architectural concrete.

above: The structural system of the HiLo floor is a thin funicular vault made of unreinforced concrete, stiffened by a system of fins on its extrados and supported at its four corners by the primary structural frame. Connected by tension ties to absorb the horizontal thrusts of the funicular shell, the solution results in a thickness of only 2 centimetres (0.8 inches) for both vault and fins.

HiLo demonstrates the use of diaphragm-stiffened shells to extend the expressive language of the project while simultaneously following a logic that produces quantifiable savings. This unification is visible even in the pattern of the ribs on the floor vault, which was inspired by the ribbed masonry vaults of the past.

Designing shell structures is not only a matter of efficiency, but also of appropriateness – of materials, space, form, energy, cost and so on. Complex, intricate designs such as spiral shell staircases in which the landings smoothly transition to become the shells of roofs or floors are not far away. Such dreams are not merely fanciful diversions; they could become practical and efficient structures combining the complex curved geometries of Parametricism's methodology with the logic offered by advances in shell construction, an opportunity to be more than just a skin.[5] △

Notes
1. Email communication with the author, 11 August 2015.
2. Eladio Dieste, 1997, as quoted in Remo Pedreschi, *Eladio Dieste: The Engineer's Contribution to Contemporary Architecture,* Thomas Telford Publishing (London), 2000, p 21.
3. Heinz Isler, 'New Shapes for Shells', International Colloquium on Construction Processes of Shell Structures, *IASS Bulletin,* 8, paper 3C, 1959, unpaginated.
4. Philippe Block, 'Thrust Network Analysis: Exploring Three-Dimensional Equilibrium', PhD dissertation, Massachusetts Institute of Technology Department of Architecture, 2009.
5. Thanks to Dr Noelle Paulson for her help with this chapter.

COMPUTATIONAL MATERIAL CULTURE

Achim Menges

Institute for Computational Design
(Achim Menges) and Institute of
Building Structures and Structural
Design (Jan Knippers),
ICD/ITKE Research Pavilion 2010,
University of Stuttgart,
2010

The pavilion's envelope consists of wooden lamellas formed by an intricate network of bent and tensioned segments. This self-equilibrating system physically computes the shape of the pavilion during assembly on site.

Computation offers considerable possibilities for architecture, going well beyond the conventional sphere of design that focuses on the generation of complex geometries. **Achim Menges**, a regular contributor and guest-editor to Δ, and Founding Director of the Institute for Computational Design (ICD) at the University of Stuttgart, is renowned for his pioneering approach to computation and materials. He describes how computation is enabling a convergence of the processes of form generation and materialisation, hailing in new areas of architectural speculation and experimentation, as demonstrated by the ICD/ITKE pavilions illustrated here.

Architecture provides the material context within which most of our everyday life unfolds. As a material practice it effectuates social, cultural and ecological relevance through the articulation of the built environment. This articulation is intrinsically tied to the processes of intellectual and physical production in which architecture originates: the processes of design and materialisation. Today, the reciprocal effects of these two processes on each other can be seen through a different lens, and computation constitutes a critical factor for this contemporary reassessment of the relation between the generation and the materialisation of form and space.

On the one hand, computation enables architects to engage facets of the material world that previously lay far outside the designer's intuition and insight. On the other, it is increasingly understood that – in its broader definition – computation is not limited to processes that operate only in the digital domain. Instead, it has been recognised that material processes also obtain a computational capacity – the ability to physically compute form. When seen together, these two aspects suggest that we are now in a position to rethink the material in architecture through the computational. As the material ambience emanating from architecture represents a critical constituent of material culture, this essay seeks to inject this notion – usually reserved for historical thought – with a projective capacity by introducing a design approach that integrates materiality and materialisation as active drivers.

DESIGN COMPUTATION: MATERIAL INTEGRATION

Over the last two decades, digital processes have had an unprecedented impact on architecture. The computer has pervaded all aspects of the discipline, from the inception of design at an early stage, to the management of building information, all the way through to fabrication and execution on site. However, the underlying conception and logic of established processes more often than not remained largely unchallenged during this adaption of new technologies, rendering them a mere computerised extension of the well known. In areas that are primarily concerned with an increase in productivity, efficiency and accuracy, this may be expected, if not particularly satisfying intellectually. But in design, with its intrinsic striving for innovation that is in sync with technological and cultural developments, it is surprising to see how often digital processes have been absorbed in the discipline without questioning traditional modes of conceiving form, structure and space.

A striking example of this languishment is the primacy of geometry in design that has dominated architectural thinking since the Renaissance and has not changed much in the transition from the manually drawn to the digitally drafted, parametrically generated or computationally derived. From a methodological point of view, this deeply entrenched prioritisation of the generation of geometric shape over the processes of material formation imbues most digital design approaches with a deeply conventional touch, even when well camouflaged in exotic form and exuberant articulation.

If, in contrast, we begin to view the computational realm not as separate from the physical domain, but instead as inherently related, we can overcome one of the greatest yet most popular misconceptions about the computer in architectural circles, namely that it is just another tool.[1] We need to embrace the computer as a significant technological development, one that offers the possibility of a novel material culture rather than just another architectural style. In the same way as 'the early moderns used the telescope and the microscope, to engage aspects of nature whose logic and pattern had previously remained ungraspable because they were lodged at too great a remove from the modalities of human sense', as Sanford Kwinter aptly puts it,[2] today architects can employ computation to delve deeper into the complex characteristics of the material world and activate them as an agency for design. In other words, through computation material no longer needs to be conceived as a passive receptor of predefined form as in established approaches, but instead can be rethought and explored as an active participant in design.

Of course, material-specific design is by no means an extraordinary thought or even a new idea. In fact, most architects would probably claim that their design decisions are directly linked to intended materiality. But usually the relation between form, space, structure and material is locked in the aforementioned hierarchy and follows an established set of preconceived rules. These 'dos and don'ts' are assumed to correspond with a constructional 'can and can't', and in the case of the modernist's truth to materials, a 'should and must not' that carries a strong moral overtone that still resonates in many architectural schools. Most often, these implicit design conventions are expressed typologically, whereby material characteristics are thought to directly relate to a set of constructional, spatial or structural typologies.

Probably the most famous example of such an assumption, still frequently glorified by architectural practitioners and academics alike, is Louis Kahn equating the will of brick with the structural typology of the arch. Today, one would hope, we can steer clear of such a one-sided conversation based on prejudged interpretation. When listening to brick, computation would have been a good hearing-aid to gain a more differentiated, multifaceted and open-ended understanding of material characteristics and their latent design potential. Instead of relating material property to constructional form based on direct and linear rules, and in contrast to the unquestioned application of preconceived construction-handbook knowledge, computation enables us to employ material behaviours and materialisation processes as a truly explorative agency in design, in which novel material, structural and spatial effects may originate.

Questioning the conventional hierarchy of form generation and materialisation, as well as the established typological approach to material-oriented design, has been a central area of study at the Institute for Computational Design (ICD) at the University of Stuttgart.[3] While this research aims at contributing insights to disciplinary concerns of architecture, the integrative nature of the approach requires interdisciplinary collaboration with various partners from engineering and natural sciences, most frequently with the university's Institute of Building Structures and Structural Design (ITKE). Over the last few years, these investigations have been conducted and tested through a series of full-scale pavilions and demonstrator buildings. Several examples of the related research and design works are presented below.

One initial area of research focused on employing the relatively well known yet architecturally largely unexplored material behaviour of elastic (de)formation. This simple form of material computation – the self-forming output of an elastic curve based on the input of the application of a given force at one support point – allows for spatially articulating initially planar elements while at the same time increasing the capacity of such a bending active structure.[4] As even this simple material behaviour cannot be conventionally drawn or modelled, it has only rarely been employed in architecture. However, today's technical possibility to compute form in unison with material characteristics enables tapping into the fascinating design potential that elastic material behaviour may offer both spatially and structurally.

The ICD/ITKE Research Pavilion 2010 pursued such an investigation through an intricate wood lamella system.[5] During assembly, these initially planar elements are connected at differential length intervals so that they form tensioned and elastically bent regions along one wooden strip that are locked into position by the adjacent strips. The distribution of the joint points between the strips oscillates along the torus shape, and this morphological irregularity results in both significant global stability and a distinctive articulation of the pavilion's envelope, which is at the same time skin and structure. Here, form and material are inherently and inseparably related, and this not only applies to the design process, but also the construction procedure where even on site the material physically computes the shape of the pavilion.

The resulting intricate network of bent and tensioned segments that form this self-equilibrating structure is perceived through the sinewy delicacy of the extremely thin wood lamellas. The residual stresses, which are embedded in the strip elements during assembly and are a decisive factor in the structural capacity of the system, form part of the visual and spatial experience through the varying undulations of the envelope, which at the same mediates a gentle transition from direct to indirect illumination that accentuates the depth of the toroidal space. The pavilion offers a glimpse of the design potential dormant in even the simplest material elements, and how this can be teased out as formerly unexplored architectural possibilities when focusing the computational process on material behaviour rather than on geometric shape. In the case of this pavilion, material is no longer just a passive receptor of predefined form, but rather becomes an active generator of design.

Institute for Computational Design (Achim Menges) and Institute of Building Structures and Structural Design (Jan Knippers), ICD/ITKE Research Pavilion 2010, University of Stuttgart, 2010

below left: The undulations of the thin wood lamellas, which are at the same time the pavilion's skin and structure, lead to differentiated direct and indirect illumination that accentuates the spatial depth.

below right: The residual stresses embedded in the building elements during assembly, which are a decisive factor in the structural capacity of the system, are experienced through the sinewy delicacy of the extremely thin wood lamellas.

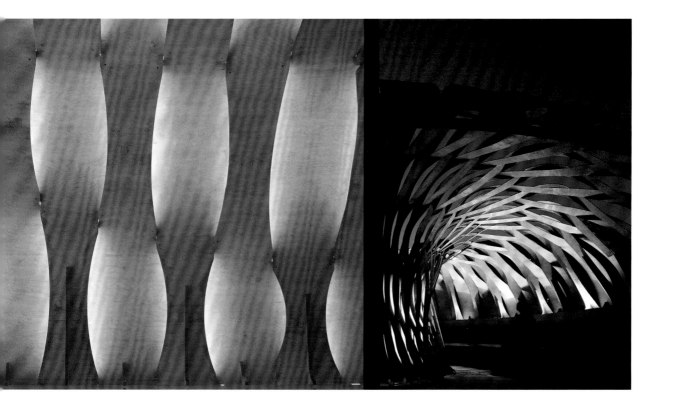

The profound impact of integrating the characteristics of material behaviour and materialisation processes in computational design thinking and techniques also allows for enriching material systems that have hitherto been considered 'amorphic' with novel morphological and tectonic possibilities. Amorphic refers to materials that are seen as 'shapeless' and thus require an external shaping device such as a mould or formwork. Concrete is a familiar example, but also fibre-composite materials such as glass- or carbon-fibre reinforced plastics (GRP/CRP) are commonly understood in this way by architects, designers and engineers alike. Based on a higher-level integration of computational design, simulation and fabrication, the ICD and ITKE have investigated an alternative approach to conceptualising and constructing fibre-composite systems in architecture that no longer relies on elaborate moulds or mandrels.[6] The goal of the study is twofold: on a technological research level, it aims to reduce the considerable effort, waste and investment involved in the fabrication of moulds, which currently renders the applications of GRP and CRP systems only suitable for the serial production of identical building elements or for application in projects with extraordinary budgetary means. On a design research level, the investigation at the same time seeks to question the common conception of fibrous composites as amorphic by minimising the need for external moulds and thus teasing out the 'morphic' character of the material itself, enabling the study of architectural articulation that unfolds from the self-expression of the fibres.

The research has led to a series of further research pavilions that are all based on constructional principles culled from the vast pool of biological composite systems. This remains a strongly tangible quality of the resulting architectural morphologies, as does the integrative approach to the computational generation and robotic materialisation of the fibrous forms. For example, in the ICD/ITKE Research Pavilion 2012, the computational approach allowed for choreographing the interaction of sequentially applied fibres through a robotic fabrication process.[7] Here, only a simple, linear scaffold is required for the filament winding, as the initial fibre layers become an embedded mould. During the production process, the application of fibres in conjunction with the pre-stress induced by the robot continuously (de)forms the system so that the final shape emerges only at the very end.

Computation not only allows understanding and deploying this complex fibrous behaviour in design, it also enables the strategic differentiation of fibre layout, organisation and density of fibres. In the resulting translucent composite surfaces of the 2012 pavilion, the black carbon rovings provide a distinctive visual reference to this intricate interplay between the fabrication- and force-driven fibre arrangements. While the constructional logic is revealed in this way, it avoids a simple and singular reading. Very different to the typical, glossy gel coat finishes stemming from moulding processes that dominate our experience of these materials, here the carbon rovings form a deep skin with a rich, layered texture. This surface texture, as well as the overall morphology and resulting novel fibrous tectonics emerge from the computationally modulated, material formation process.

Institute for Computational Design (Achim Menges) and Institute of Building Structures and Structural Design (Jan Knippers), ICD/ITKE Research Pavilion 2012, University of Stuttgart, 2012

left: The form of the pavilion's composite shell gradually emerges through the interaction of fibres applied on a minimal scaffold during a robotic filament-winding process. Computation allows for understanding this complex material behaviour in design and enables the strategic differentiation of fibre layout, organisation and density of fibres, resulting in novel fibrous tectonics.

opposite left: The pavilion's skin-structure is an extremely thin composite shell that does not require any additional support elements. In the translucent glass-fibre surfaces, the black carbon rovings provide a distinctive visual reference to the intricate interplay between the fabrication- and force-driven fibre arrangements.

right: The glass- and carbon-fibre rovings form a deep skin with a rich, layered texture that emerges from the computationally modulated material-formation process.

The profound impact of integrating the characteristics of material behaviour and materialisation processes in computational design thinking and techniques also allows for enriching material systems that have hitherto been considered 'amorphic' with novel morphological and tectonic possibilities.

More recently, the research has been expanded towards cyber-physical production systems, in which the fabrication machine is no longer dependent on receiving a comprehensive and finite set of manufacturing instructions, but instead has the sensorial ability to gather information from its fabrication environment and change its production behaviour in real time.[8] Here, machine and material computation become fully synthesised in an open-ended process. In the ICD/ITKE Research Pavilion 2014–15 this approach allowed for gradually hardening an initially soft – and thus continuously deforming – inflated envelope by applying fibres on the inside. Eventually, a structurally stable state was reached so that the internal air pressure could be released and the pneumatic envelope changed into the pavilion's skin. In daylight, there remains only a subtle trace of the fibrous structure on the reflective envelope from the outside, which transforms into an expressive texture when illuminated from within at night. On the inside, the initial softness of the roving bundles remains tangible in the fibres' texture, which strongly contrasts with their actually hardened state. This evokes at the same time a strong sense of transparency and even airiness, as well as a stringy leanness and tangible tautness of the extremely lightweight structure.

EMERGING MATERIAL CULTURE

The projects introduced above begin to suggest how material performance and architectural performativity can be synthesised in ways that go far beyond a trite truth to materials and related fixed and singular structural and spatial typologies. The computational convergence of the processes of form generation and materialisation enables new modes of architectural speculation and experimentation that will contribute to the definition of a truly contemporary, computational material culture, which also constitutes an important facet and ambition of Parametricism 2.0. A humble indication of the potential richness of such an integrative design approach may be given by the pavilion examples illustrated here, which all stem from one coherent body of design research yet display a considerable variety in formal, spatial and structural articulation. △

Institute for Computational
Design (Achim Menges) and
Institute of Building Structures
and Structural Design (Jan
Knippers),
ICD/ITKE Research Pavilion
2014-15,
University of Stuttgart,
2015

opposite top left: Computational design, simulation and fabrication enable a synthesis of structure and skin that is perceived differently on the interior and exterior of the pavilion. During the day, only a subtle trace of the fibrous structure is visible on the reflective envelope, whereas the stark contrast between the transparent skin and the black carbon is strongly perceived on the inside.

opposite bottom left: The interior of the pavilion reveals the intricate carbon-fibre structure that articulates the spatial surface and at the same time provides the structural support for the transparent – and initially inflated – ETFE envelope.

left: At night, the constructional logic of the cyber-physical design and fabrication approach remains tangible in the distinctive architectural articulation of the pavilion.

Notes
1. Sanford Kwinter, 'Cooking, Yo-ing, Thinking', *Tarp: Not Nature*, Pratt Institute (New York), 2012, p 108.
2. Sanford Kwinter, 'The Computational Fallacy', in Achim Menges and Sean Ahlquist, *Computational Design Thinking*, John Wiley & Sons (London), 2011, pp 211–15.
3. Achim Menges, 'Material Resourcefulness: Activating Material Information', in Achim Menges (ed), △ *Material Computation*, March/April (no 2), 2012, pp 34–43.
4. Julian Lienhard, Simon Schleicher and Jan Knippers, 'Bending-Active Structures: Research Pavilion ICD/ITKE', in David Nethercot and Sergio Pellegrino *et al* (eds), *Proceedings of the International Symposium of the IABSE-IASS Symposium, Taller Longer Lighter*, IABSE-IASS Publications (London), 2011.
5. Moritz Fleischmann, Jan Knippers, Julian Lienhard, Achim Menges and Simon Schleicher, 'Material Behaviour: Embedding Physical Properties in Computational Design Processes', in Achim Menges (ed), △ *Material Computation*, March/April (no 2), 2012, pp 44–51.
6. Achim Menges and Jan Knippers, 'Fibrous Tectonics', in Achim Menges (ed), △ *Material Synthesis*, September/October (no 5), 2015, pp 40–47.
7. Steffen Reichert, Tobias Schwinn, Riccardo La Magna, Frédéric Waimer, Jan Knippers and Achim Menges, 'Fibrous Structures: An Integrative Approach to Design Computation, Simulation and Fabrication for Lightweight, Glass and Carbon Fibre Composite Structures in Architecture Based on Biomimetic Design Principles', *CAD Journal*, 52, July 2014, pp 27–39.
8. Achim Menges, 'The New Cyber-Physical Making in Architecture: Computational Construction', in Achim Menges (ed), △ *Material Synthesis*, September/October (no 5), 2015, pp 28–33.

Enriqueta Llabres
and Eduardo Rico

Relational Urban Models

Parameters, Values and Tacit Forms of Algorithms

Parameter-dependent processes have huge potential for urban design and planning, which is shaped by the relational input of a number of parties or stakeholders. **Enriqueta Llabres and Eduardo Rico** of the multidisciplinary London-based office Relational Urbanism describe how they have developed participatory urban models that translate data into parameters, bringing to the fore the influences of shared relational values.

The advent of digital technologies and the resulting array of available techniques for capturing and interpreting data have shifted the ways in which we look at and analyse the urban domain. Perhaps if this current scenario is distinctive, it is because it empowers people to organise themselves and take on a more proactive role in the decisions that affect their immediate environment. New forms of digital urban documents are emerging that collate input from designers, government bodies and members of the public, allowing information sharing and feedback from the end user to the design team and vice versa. This has implications for practitioners using digital models where rules are introduced in a relational perspective by different agents. This form of shared authorship makes possible interventions where architectural design, development policies and participation are intertwined, opening up spatial regimes in which continuity and differentiation are deployed in the model in unexpected ways.

Proposed here is a new design approach to digital forms of urban documentation based on Relational Urban Models (RUMs) developed by the multidisciplinary practice Relational Urbanism. The article describes how the translation of data into parameters, values and tacit forms of algorithms ties in with a relational understanding of space and time, and how this has been deployed in three different projects in China and Brazil. The first two RUMs, in Baishizhou village in Shenzhen and Santos in São Paulo, were research projects awarded in the Arup Global Research challenge competition 2013-Call3 and later developed jointly by Relational Urbanism, Arup and Immanuel Koh, RU Coding Director. The third, for a riverbed, was developed by Relational Urbanism as part of the Back to Future City Workshop at the 403 International Art Centre in Wuhan, Hubei province.

New digital forms of urban documentation are now becoming commonplace on the Internet. An example is Abu Dhabi Blue Carbon Demonstration Project,[1] led by the emirate's Global Environmental Data Initiative and Environment Agency. Using an online model, it calculates the carbon sequestration capacity of a specific biomass within an area selected by the user, showcasing it against the different components of the chosen ecosystem. The tool is shared in the Blue Carbon Portal, an online community that disseminates scientific research, policy instruments and market applications regarding the conservation of 'blue carbon' – the capacity of coastal ecosystems and oceans to perform as carbon sinks. Another example is the Smart Citizen initiative in Barcelona,[2] where individuals can use open-source technology to upload live data about the air quality in their community that then remains publicly accessible. Both of these schemes generate awareness of certain issues and act as checks on environmental governance, but more importantly they point to a key challenge in digital design – the question of how data (either formal or environmental) can start to build shared values.

Parameters are bounded to define a particular system from which a quantity is selected according to specific circumstances and in relation to which other variables might be expressed. Values point to the fact that something is held to deserve its importance or worth of something for someone. Both parameters and values are relative, but while a parameter is relative to an established system, a value is relative to individuals. In urban design, space, time and value are intimately intertwined, and turning parameters into values is therefore the most critical issue at stake in urban parametric models.

In this sense, the urban geographer David Harvey distinguishes between two ways of constructing space, time and value: social and relational.[3] A social construction is imposed by the established mechanisms of social reproduction, dictated by elites and implemented through forms of direct or indirect social control such as urban protocols, regulations and the media. A relational construction understands that it is possible to have multiple constructions coming from different groups of people that share similar values. These groups, which Harvey calls 'domains', are relative to the particular issue at stake and can share common features such as disciplinary background, gender or ethnicity. A relational construction of space, time and value implies a tension, a negotiation between these different domains.

Another implication that comes from relating parameters to values is that a parameter constitutes a form of knowledge that is explicit and codified, while values hold a tacit dimension. The definition of the tacit dimension was introduced in the 1960s by the British-Hungarian polymath Michael Polanyi, who is renowned for his theoretical contributions to physical chemistry, economics and philosophy. Initially referring to production in the creative arts, the tacit dimension is characterised by knowledge that can be conceptualised and transmitted before it can be explicitly rationalised. The designer often has to engage with this level of knowledge and reach the wider audience through inner feelings and developing ideas in the form of intuition that can only be contained within the individual.

These two characteristics – the relational construction of space, time and value and the tacit dimension – are what underpin Relational Urbanism's development of RUMs. These customised toolkits of urban parametric models, databases, infographics and interactive platforms allow real-time interplay with urban form in such a way that the design team can work on interdependencies between different spatial and non-spatial components of an urban project. The purpose is not so much to showcase existing data or decisions made a priori, but fabricating new knowledge and building urban institutions understood as 'a set of rules based on ethical values of a specific community that influence the individual's decision making'.[4]

In this context, design has a critical role giving the construction of space, time and value significance and 'designating its relation to other things, owners, users, or goods. Based on this original meaning, one could say: design is making sense (of things).'[5] It is therefore the task of the designer to understand both the target audience and the project in order to strike a balance between parameters, values and tacit forms of algorithms.

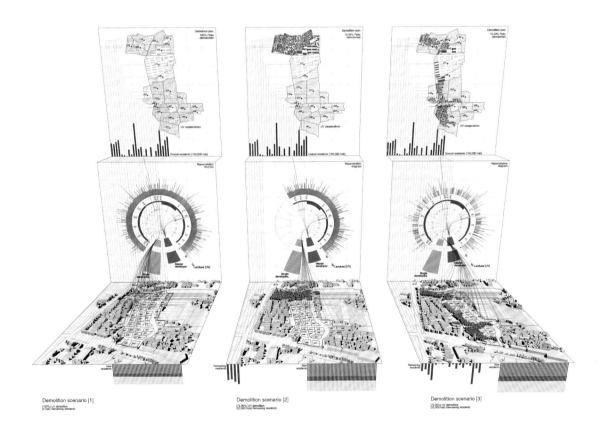

Demolition scenario [1]

Demolition scenario [2]

Demolition scenario [3]

Relational Urbanism, Arup and Immanuel Koh, RU Coding Director, Baishizhou RUM, Baishizhou, Shenzhen, China, 2014

Relational model outcome for three demolition options. Existing plots were grouped by owner cooperatives that were granted development rights and linked to footfall. The option retaining more of the existing fabric (bottom right) shows a greater urban mix.

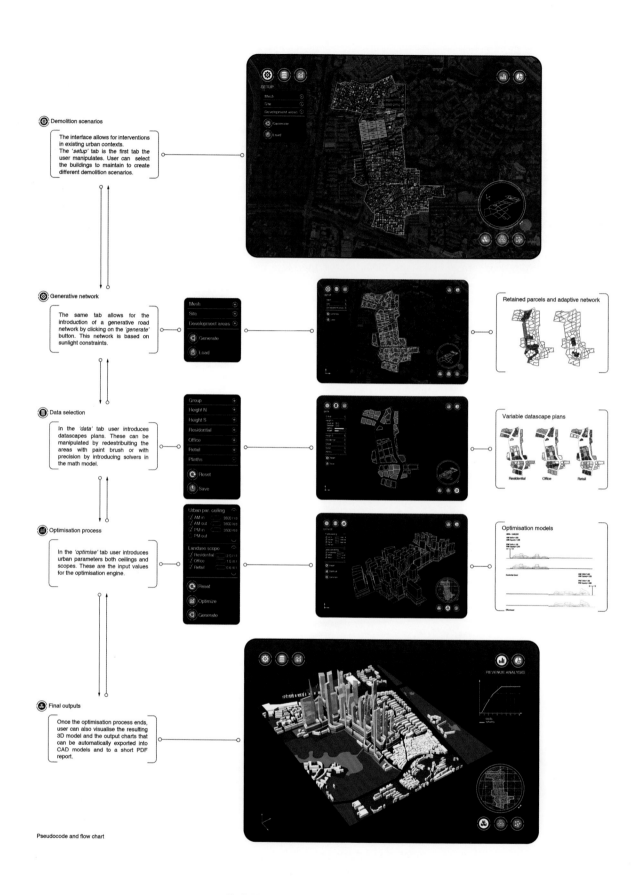

Demolition scenarios

The interface allows for interventions in existing urban contexts. The *'setup'* tab is the first tab the user manipulates. User can select the buildings to maintain to create different demolition scenarios.

Generative network

The same tab allows for the introduction of a generative road network by clicking on the *'generate'* button. This network is based on sunlight constraints.

Retained parcels and adaptive network

Data selection

In the *'data'* tab user introduces datascapes plans. These can be manipulated by redistributing the areas with paint brush or with precision by introducing solvers in the math model.

Variable datascape plans

Residential   Office   Retail

Optimisation process

In the *'optimise'* tab user introduces urban parameters both ceilings and scopes. These are the input values for the optimisation engine.

Optimisation models

Final outputs

Once the optimisation process ends, user can also visualise the resulting 3D model and the output charts that can be automatically exported into CAD models and to a short PDF report.

Pseudocode and flow chart

The RUM as a negotiation device. The model allowed users to navigate through demolition options and design studies (density, land use distribution and grouping) before introducing urban parameters (thresholds and scopes) for each round of optimisation.

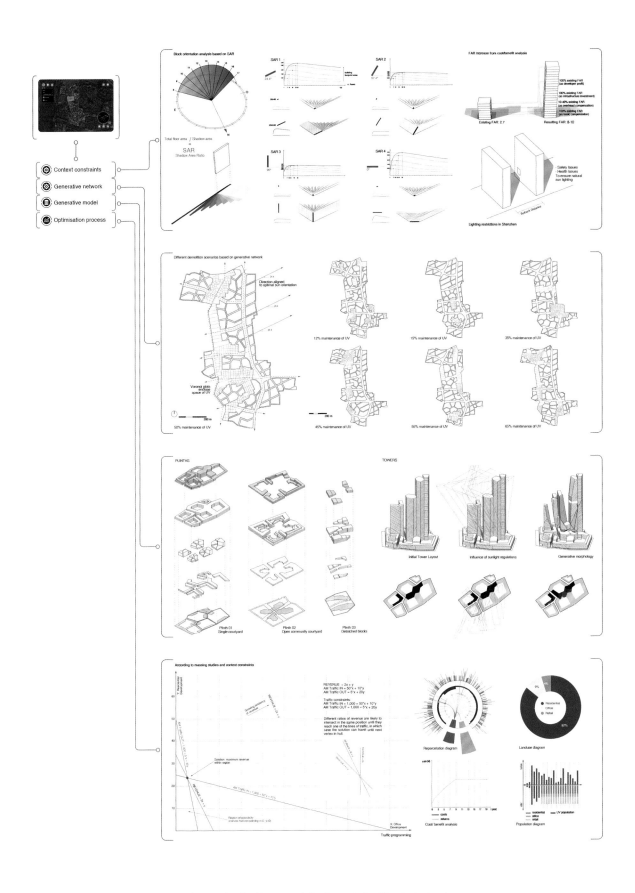

A generative algorithm responded to the proximity of the street network to retained blocks. The morphology of the resulting urban network and plinths allowed for a diversity of public spaces that expanded from intimate courtyards to urban parks, while the final morphology of towers was sculpted above by constraints of sunlight exposure.

Baishizhou RUM, Shenzhen

The first RUM was designed to be a negotiation device between master developers and urban municipalities for densification plans in the context of urban villages in Shenzhen. The model was developed in 2014 by Relational Urbanism and Arup with the support of Shenzhen University and local NGOs. In this case, the RUM was designed to be used mainly by a small group of stakeholders with clear targets. It worked as a generative platform comparing quality of space, cost-benefit analysis and social mix; acting on the one hand as a negotiation device between the municipality and the master developers, and on the other as an instrument to generate urban form.

The negotiation device focused on a local government initiative to retain sufficient low-cost accommodation across Shenzhen to house key workers in urban villages such as Baishizhou. This policy clashes with the expectations of landowners and master developers whose aim is to replace the existing fabric with upgraded, denser and therefore more profitable schemes. The model allowed the user to input scopes and constraints. Scopes were different portions of urban village to retain, land-use distribution across the site and the distribution of architectural solutions. Constraints were maximum traffic, morning and night, in and out. In each test, the model provided as output the cost-benefit analysis, the amount of public space and retail at the ground level. In this way, options such as partial demolition could be explored simultaneously with an understanding of the financial implications for the master developer.

The main task of the Baishizhou RUM was thus to envision forms of incremental regeneration that partially maintain the social mix. The street network was introduced as a generative algorithm that responds to the proximity of retained parts of the urban village, emphasising the value of existing public spaces. The architectural solution aimed to provide a rich diversity of public spaces that would gradually blend the close and intimate urban squares dominant in urban villages with the modern residential towers. A generative morphology of tower plinths allowed this diversity, while the final morphology of the towers that emerged above was constrained by the volume of space that had to remain unbuilt for the residential land uses to comply with Shenzhen's lighting regulations. These regulations have historically made partial interventions in urban villages difficult as new buildings need to be spaced far apart to accommodate the densities that the master developer requires. This condition has led urban villages to stagnate until a single major developer regenerates the overall area, often resulting in just a new version of the much-criticised late-Modernist scheme. To overcome this trend, the model allowed the free positioning of the tower footprints, with the resulting envelope morphology complying with the city's lighting regulations.

An optimisation mechanism was used to interrupt and reverse the flow of information that typically starts with the design parameters and ends with the calculation results. The outputs can therefore be turned into inputs, seamlessly moving between spatial, infrastructural and economic decisions, and opening up discussions about the marginal costs of design concepts and potential economic transfers linked to density distribution.

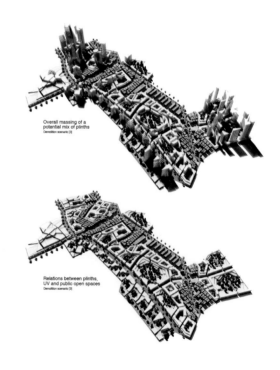

Sample of plan and 3D view for Baishizhou regeneration project, Shenzhen, China, 2014

Mixed outcome of plinths and plinths plus towers (left) together with ground-floor plan (right). The use of RUMs emphasises qualities of texture and urban grain, opening up discussions on the relationships between specific details such as the encounter with the existing fabric and generic ones for wider regimes of landscape architecture proposals.

Overall, the Baishizhou RUM was designed so that the users were able to control the parameters systematically rather than intuitively looking for a balance between the social mix and profit. This produced a series of demolition options, all of which created a similar new development area but had different spatial results and implications on social mix. The model succeeded in finding urban design solutions that could be beneficial to master developers while partially maintaining urban villages, meeting cost-benefit expectations and providing a continuous yet diverse spectrum of urban blocks and public spaces that responds to the context.

Santos RUM, São Paulo

The second research project was developed by Relational Urbanism and Arup in 2014 and involved the application of a RUM in the renewal of a low-density, light-industrial and residential area in the Villanova and Paqueta districts of Santos municipality in São Paulo. The urban fabric was dominated by small residential plots, mostly terraced houses with narrow frontages and large courtyards to the inside of the blocks. The two districts are currently undergoing a transformation driven by public investment in civic buildings and two new tramlines, however this also required the introduction of public space. In this case, the RUM was designed as a policy instrument to incentivise landowners to cluster the small blocks into larger ones and thus release ground for the public spaces.

The main challenge was orchestrating the diverse proposals to create an overall identity and coherent character for the area without relying on a single masterplan that dictated the final urban form. In this context, the RUM was designed to be used by a small group of landowners with different backgrounds. The main input data was which land parcels would be grouped together. Based on individual values rather than established parameters, this data could not be predicted by the design team and needed to be captured by the designers and mediated through incentives set by the municipality.

An important aspect of the RUM here was testing the effects on the existing urban fabric of an incentive that called for increased building heights and the introduction of new architectural solutions. The model tested densities as well as the impact of the floor-to-area ratio (FAR) bonus for landscape provision, giving rapid feedback on the influence of the policy to provide public space together with a vision of the quality and diversity of programmes that could be introduced. Overall, the Santos RUM catered for individual decisions regarding clustering and the reaching of one-to-one agreements. Design tests and iterations were more difficult to systematise and input data needed to be captured in the form of values about preferences in pooling resources by members of the public.

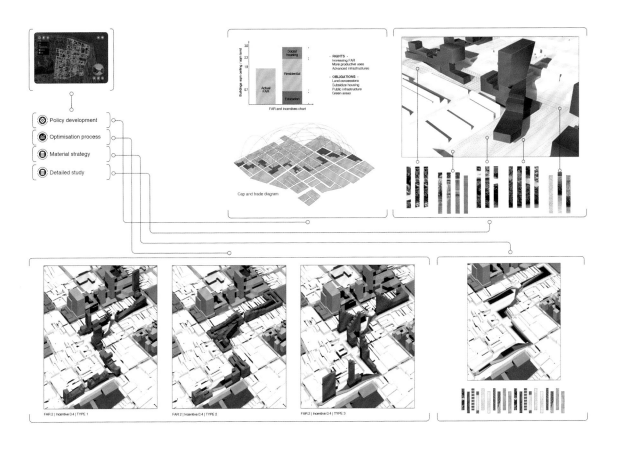

Relational Urbanism, Arup and Immanuel Koh, RU Coding Director, Santos RUM, Santos, São Paulo, Brazil, 2014

The RUM here was a generative urban landscape linked to a policy instrument to incentivise the regeneration and creation of public space. The parametric proposal related buildings to open space to provide high-density solutions while driving pedestrians through the core of the block as a way of promoting diagonal forms of circulation in an otherwise solely orthogonal grid. Selected blocks are threaded through a local system of public space to allow the trading of land use, selection of urban morphologies and investment levels to obtain a greater floor-to-area ratio (FAR).

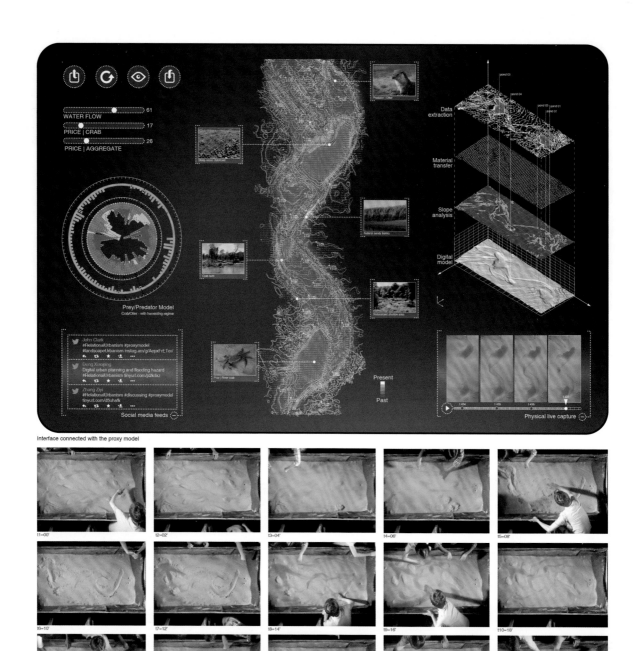

Interface connected with the proxy model

Live capture frames

Relational Urbanism, Riverbed RUM, Wuhan, China, 2014

The physical model in this installation for the Back to Future City Workshop in Wuhan was digitally captured using a laser level for the overall slope and colour coding for water depth. Data from the physical model was analysed and inputted into ecological and economic models that were coordinated and projected in real time. Further development speculated on the construction of a Web-based interface.

Riverbed RUM, Wuhan

The tacit dimension of the RUM was further emphasised in the last project. Here it was dominated by intuitive forms of material engagement with the general public, captured and exposed by the Relational Urbanism design team using a live physical model and a digital interface. The aim was to raise awareness of the problems of sediment and ecosystem management in river landscapes. This is particularly relevant in Wuhan, where the Yangtze and Han Rivers meet. Two of the most important rivers in China, both have suffered high degrees of human intervention due to the construction of large dams, canalisation for flood protection purposes as well as sediment extraction from their banks for use as aggregate in the construction industry. All these interventions have both spatial and ecological implications, which the installation wanted to showcase.

The RUM in this case performed an interactive river simulation in which the user introduced live changes in the physical model and could then observe their morphological, ecological and economic evolution in real time. A scaled-down version of a braided river ran constantly in a laboratory tank where both water and sediment were dropped in the upper part of the model in order to allow the current to morph small-scale beaches, braids or abandoned channels within a short amount of time. The results of the model were of a qualitative nature and its main characteristic was the idea of 'play' as a form of tacit algorithm; the causes and effects of human actions are amplified and accelerated so the spectator becomes aware of the interdependencies, subtleties and relational nature of the environment in which he or she is manufacturing. Here, the tacit component of the RUM seeks to immerse itself in the river dynamics provided by the texture and noise of the model as well as the data projections.

Parameters, Values and Tacit Forms of Algorithms

In the three Relational Urbanism projects described above, the data underpinning the RUMs migrates from parameters to values and tacit forms of algorithms. This is made possible by the degree of openness and participation now offered by digital design technologies, generating relational forms of spatial knowledge. While in Baishizhou the spatial outcome shows continuous but differentiated components driven by a clear set of parameters, in Santos accidents and unpredictable discontinuities are possible as continuity can only be guaranteed through the sharing of common values, which in this case are embedded in the landscape and materials used for creating the new public space. However, introducing a tacit dimension into the parametric models can create new forms of spatial culture and appreciation for the texture of the city that can be incorporated in the development of plans and policies. In this context, urban designers need to calibrate the introduction of parameters, values and tacit forms of algorithms, and become aware of the entire architectural cultures, producing both continuities and differentiations, that ultimately form the character of our cities. △

Notes
1. See bluecarbonportal.org/abu-dhabi-blue-carbon-demonstration-project/.
2. See https://smartcitizen.me.
3. David Harvey, *Justice, Nature and the Geography of Difference*, Wiley-Blackwell (Oxford), 1996.
4. Douglass North, *Institutions, Institutional Change and Economic Performance*, Cambridge University Press (Cambridge), 1990.
5. Roberto Verganti, 'Design, Meanings and Radical Innovation. A Metamodel and a Research Agenda', *Journal of Product Innovation Management*, 25, 5, 2006: pp 436–56.

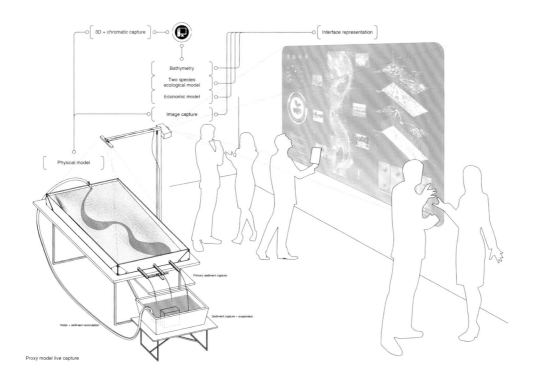

Interaction between public and watercourse in a physical relational model. Users could manually sculpt islands and pools for the river model to slowly morph into alternative landscapes. The model showed qualitative similarity in terms of water and sediment flow with large-scale counterparts of braided and anastomosising rivers.

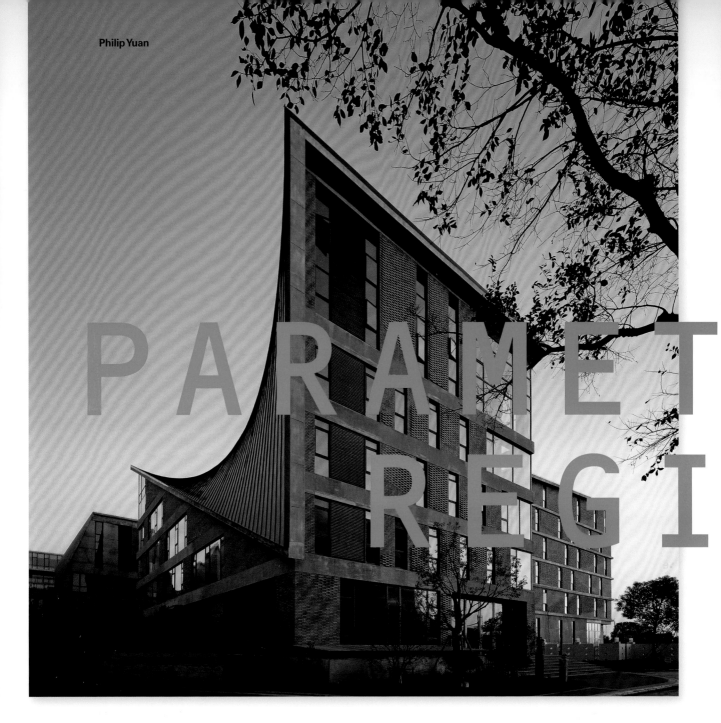

PARAMET
REGI

Archi-Union Architects,
Songjiang Art Campus,
Shanghai,
2015

The offsetting logic of the brick
pattern becomes a simple
numbering and positioning logic,
which is easy and economical for
the builders to interpret.

Philip Yuan, Founding Director of Shanghai-based firm Archi-Union Architects, applies parametric techniques to his design and research in China. Here he explains how Parametricism can provide a highly adaptive and open approach to architectural knowledge and spatial organisation, accommodating regional variations in culture and environment, through an emphasis on local climate, materials and craft traditions.

Adaptability is the very core of Parametricism, which feeds off technological transformation and thrives on change. Not limited to technique alone, adaptation in parametric design can be extended to respond to regional specifics and variations. Using computational technology, the architect applies an integrated design methodology through the exploration of the specific meanings of various architectural parameters such as material performance, building tectonics and human behaviour.

Regionalism is not only reflected in the local context and climate, but also inherent in cultural aspects like building materials and craftsmanship. The discourse of regionalism in the digital age has broad social and ethical significance. In the past years, I have been applying parametric design methodology to my practice and research in China. This article focuses on the deployment of parameters on the performance of local materials like bricks, concrete and timber, and explores the new opportunities offered by the integration between parametric design and regional culture.

Architectural Regionalism in the Digital Era

Architecture exists within a visual, physical and social context. In the context of the information age, 'big data' not only brings us a globalised world but also provides more possibilities in reinterpreting the environment, materials, social organisation and human behaviour from a regional perspective. The instant communication between social organisation and Internet information relying on local characteristics enables the versatile and customised development of globalisation. Hence, regionalism in the context of the digital era is increasingly concerned with the integration and regeneration of physical information and virtual data through new technologies. The operation and progress of social systems always involves rich regional customs and cultural heritage, and the formation of their conventions is closely related to the local environment and social production. Parametric design provides a new approach to architectural knowledge and spatial organisation; it should incorporate regional information and local behaviour from a broad perspective.[1]

The reformation of the parametric paradigm should be the aim instead of the result. Transformation of the architectural production system, ecological ethics and human behaviour will inevitably lead to innovation in architectural morphology. Therefore, the significance of theoretical research lies more in changing the future than in predicting the future through advanced technology. The architectural design process has been significantly improved through computational thinking. In recent years, through a great deal of practice, the open discourse of parametric methodology has had a major influence on design thinking and processes. Parametric models have completely broken the boundaries between design and fabrication, enabling an integrated life-cycle design methodology from conceptualisation to operation, revision and construction through the manipulation of geometric information.[2] The logicality, flexibility, interactivity and constructability of parametric systems correspond to a fully open system of digital design and fabrication.

Through the design process of parametric methodology, the systematic significance of architectural components is enhanced. If our common ground of architecture still starts from basic building elements like the door, window, stair and elevator, as shown by Rem Koolhaas's 'Elements of Architecture' exhibition at the 2014 Venice Architecture Biennale, then the new possibility brought by parametric thinking lies in precise definition of the component with strong adaptability to environment, behaviours and material. Undoubtedly, the openness of Parametricism provides architecture with reinforced regional characteristics. Regional Parametricism embeds architectural morphology with performative aesthetics. It thus contributes to the project of parametric semiology.

Parametric prototypes build up a connection between architectural geometry and performative parameters of local climate, material, structure and behaviour. The decision as to which geometrical parameters matter in architecture becomes the key to the design approach.[3] Regional information can be directly fed into geometric parameters of building elements through purposeful selection and extraction of data. In this way, not only construction information about local materials, but also organisational instructions of building systems can be operated simultaneously with great efficiency through computational design. This innovative methodology brings the novel tectonics to help architects transform the current situation of architectural design and production to a new digital era. I would like to illustrate the exploration of digital regionalism through examples from my research and practice in recent years.

Digital Design and Fabrication of Traditional Materials

Traditional craftsmanship should not be seen only in terms of its cultural value. The significance of traditional materials will be redefined as architects pay closer attention to their performative characteristics and fabrication logics. What is more, the unique geographical features embodied in traditional materials bring rich regional characteristics into architectural design.[4] In recent years, I have devoted my architectural practice to digital fabrication using local materials. From the undulating visual effect given by the varied angles of the blocks forming the exterior surfaces of the Archi-Union Architects office in Shanghai (2011) and of the Lanxi Curtilage in Chengdu, Sichuan (2012), to the plain red brick wall of the Songjiang Art Campus in Shanghai (2015), and the raw concrete public spaces of the Tea House (2011) and Jade Museum (2013), also in Shanghai, traditional materials have been subjected to morphological experiments to achieve a creative standard of performative tectonics.

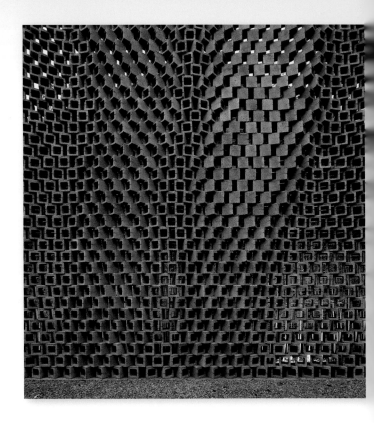

Archi-Union Architects, Silk Wall of the Archi-Union Office, Shanghai, 2011

top, centre and bottom:
The angles of rotation of the cement blocks were limited to 21 values. Wooden templates were provided by the architects to teach the builders how to allocate the blocks to the correct position.

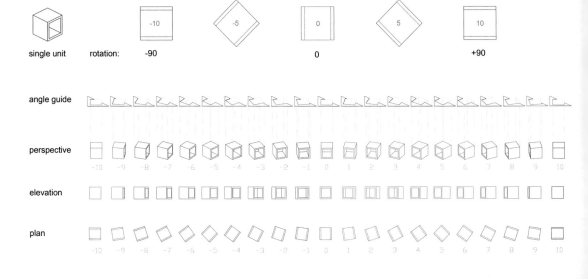

Brick Aggregation

The initial design strategy of the 'Silk Wall', the external facade of Archi-Union's office and studio, was to manipulate the gradient of the 'silk cloth' to achieve infinitely variable rotation angles of the hollow bricks. However, it would have become impossible for the builders to construct in terms of time and cost if we had not compromised by regulating the rotation angles of the bricks to 21 fixed numbers of degrees. The same technique was applied in the Lanxi Curtilage, a private clubhouse located in the intangible cultural heritage garden in Chengdu. Five types of customised offset brick joints were adapted to create the waving pattern on the wall. In Songjiang Art Campus, which was designed to accommodate studio and exhibition spaces for Shanghai contemporary artists, we again reconfigured the traditional 'Ding-Shun' (Flemish bond) brick construction method using the non-linear logic of parametric design. Simple positioning and measuring methods enable the workers to understand the construction process. The brick wall creates an effect of a gently undulating fabric-like texture. Eight convex–concave relationships have been adopted in the construction of the masonry, which not only create different textured effects on the building's elevations, but also ensure the rationality of the construction process.

On the construction site for all three of these projects, our architects provided customised positioning tools to help the builders determine the location of each brick. Although the accuracy depends upon the level of the craftsmanship, it nonetheless guarantees the integrity of the design intention and maintains the productivity and economy of construction.

The practice of brick morphology demonstrates a low-tech digital fabrication approach, which integrates computational design with local craftsmanship; it sets up a pioneering model for the reformation of regional architectural tectonics. The idea behind this low-tech digital fabrication methodology is to bridge the gap between the advanced parametric ideology of architects and the laggard constructional experience of local builders, and motivate them to create new performative architecture within the regional context.

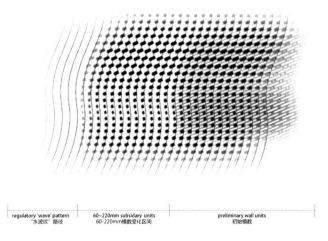

regulatory 'wave' pattern
"水波纹"路径

60~220mm subsidary units
60-220mm模数变化区间

preliminary wall units
初始模数

Archi-Union Architects,
Lanxi Curtilage,
Chengdu, China, 2012

left and right: The wavy pattern of the facade is achieved through designing different sizes of brick joints. The permutation of the joint values was then translated to a simple bricklaying process.

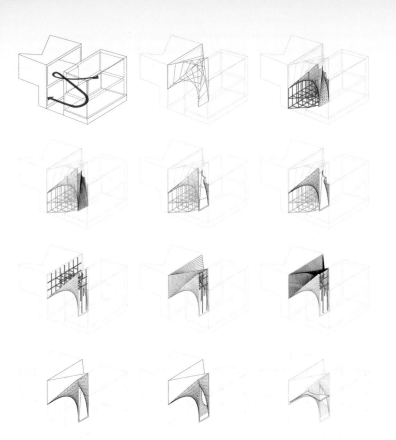

Concrete Fabrication

The Tea House is located in the backyard of Archi-Union's office and used as a library and meeting space for the architects. The transitional concrete space between its two storeys is hard to document through two-dimensional drawings. The complex geometry had to be rationalised into constructible segments. Working with the builders, we constructed a full-scale timber formwork to ensure the accuracy of the concrete pouring process. The layout of the steel reinforcement also follows the geometrical logic of ruled surface. It was Archi-Union's first attempt to combine digital fabrication techniques with local concrete construction methods. Although after completion many defects were left on the surface of the material due to the manual construction process used, these somehow reveal and reinforce the regional aesthetics of material and craftsmanship.

Inside Jade Museum, a private art museum located in Xuhui District, Shanghai, the multistorey art space is organised around a central circulation stairway that

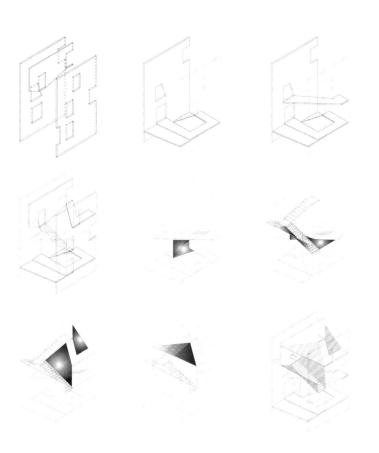

opens directly off the courtyard. The original monotonously linear floor-to-floor model of the old building was reconfigured through the design of a non-linear concrete space, where vertical and horizontal movements intersect and interact. The ambiguity of the interfaces between the different spaces creates a variegated folding and blending effect. Visitors' movement is redefined, while there is a continuous variation of integrated geometric profiles. The integration of non-linear metrics and existing geometry became the key to the design and fabrication. The multidimensional curved surfaces were abstracted and decomposed into controllable CNC-milled fragments, while the three-dimensional field splices were controlled by accurate positioning techniques. The curved profile was translated into linear construction logic under the premise of satisfying the geometric principles of the design. A spatial expression that would have been unrealisable through traditional skills has here been transferred to the sequential logic of digital fabrication processes with great accuracy, so that parametric modelling has ensured the implementation of design initiatives throughout the whole construction process.

Archi-Union Architects, Jade Museum, Shanghai, 2013

top and bottom: The multidimensional ruled surface is broken down into straight CNC panels. The combination of digital fabrication and local craftsmanship ensures quality and speed of construction without compromising the design integrity.

Archi-Union Architects, Tea House at Archi-Union Office, Shanghai, 2011

opposite top and bottom: The fabrication of the non-linear transitional space is realised through a 1:1 framework built with a series of layers of straight timber battens for concrete casting.

Timber Tectonics

In the Reverse Rafter project (2014) at Shanghai's Tongji University, the traditional wood rafter was studied and then processed and reconfigured using new structural performance modelling tools as well as robotic fabrication. In the *Yingzao Fashi* (literally *Treatise on Architectural Methods or State Building Standards*), penned by the Chinese writer Li Jie around the year 1100 and first published in 1103, there are clear instructions for the proportions of projecting rafters. We checked and refined the proportions of these rafters parametrically by using the structural performance software component Millipede and the genetic-algorithm-based optimisation tool Galapagos, both for McNeel Grasshopper®, establishing a triangular self-supporting unit through the combination of three timber members, so as to produce a new structural system. The whole structure is composed of seven units which follow the same logic. But the problem is that each individual member must be different in terms of length, angle of inclination and joint. Precise digital fabrication using five-axis CNC is proven to be reliable for this sophisticated timber construction.[5]

The idea of a modular timber structure and corresponding construction logic was then applied to some of our projects in practice. In the BaoHua Temple project in Huangzhou (2013), the traditional post-and-lintel construction was reinterpreted by computational algorithms. Every structural and decorative detail of the classic component was distilled and then reinterpreted through parametric semiology. As a result, a traditional Chinese timber temple was transformed into contemporary aesthetic architecture with embedded regional features. In the conceptual design of the Xiaoqinghe Wetland children's centre (2014), on the Xiaoqing river in Shandong province, the idea of parametric regionalism is fully explored. The centre is a fluid 50-metre-long (160-foot) sheltered timber corridor with a constantly changing sectional experience. There is no fixed dimension of structural elements. The roofs and floors evolve following the interaction between children and nature. The space, programme and structure are integrated as one parametric system, and regional timber components – columns, beams, purlins and rafters – are reconfigured into performative architectural elements that are always responsive to the local context. The flexible and sensitive system also opens up opportunities for fast and economically feasible digital fabrication processes. Every timber component can be manufactured off site and accurately assembled on site, which leaves minimal impact on the natural environment during construction.

Digital Design Research Center, College of Architecture and Urban Planning, Tongji University, Reverse Rafter, Shanghai, 2013

The sizing and proportions of the timber rafter were structurally analysed and optimised using Millipede and Galapagos in Rhinoceros Grasshopper.

A New Age of Performative Architecture

Material-performance-based design approaches emphasise close relationships between building performance and material properties.[6] Taking material research as the substance, the exploration of craftsmanship as the objective, digital design as the methodology and digital fabrication as the technique, an integrated architectural design procedure, from forming to modelling and construction, emerges.

Nowadays, the parametric paradigm is becoming an in-depth interpretation of the meaning of parameters. Using the logic of numbers, architects can apply an integrated design methodology to the discovery of specific data on aspects such as material performance, fabrication methods and human behaviour. Regionalism, meanwhile, addresses not only local craftsmanship, but also local climate, site information, local culture and behaviour. The discourse of regionalism in the digital age has a broad ethical significance. Architects in this new age are combining advanced architectural practice with traditional Chinese culture, developing performative local building materials and adaptive forms of architecture through digital design and fabrication, and exploring the new possibilities of the integration of Parametricism and regionalism through new digital craftsmanship.[7] △

Archi-Union Architects, Xiaoqinghe Wetland Children's Centre, Jinan, China, 2014

The sections indicate the constant undulation of the roofs and floors. The space, programme and structure are integrated as one parametric system, and the regional timber components – columns, beams, purlins and rafters – are reconfigured into performative parametric elements.

Notes
1. See Patrik Schumacher, *The Autopoiesis of Architecture*, Vol I: *A New Framework of Architecture*, John Wiley & Sons (Chichester), 2011, pp 5–8.
2. See Bob Sheil and Ruairi Glynn, *Fabricate: Making Digital Architecture*, Riverside Architectural Press (Toronto), 2012, pp 30–35.
3. See Michael Hensel, Defne Sunguroglu and Achim Menges, 'Material Performance', △ *Versatility and Vicissitude: Performance in Morpho-Ecological Design*, March/April (no 2), 2008, pp 34–41.
4. See Antoine Picon, *Digital Culture in Architecture*, Birkhäuser (Basel), 2010, pp 30–35.
5. See Philip F Yuan, Hyde Meng, Zhang Liming, 'New Craftsmanship Using Traditional Materials', in Philip F Yuan, Achim Menges and Neil Leach (eds), *Robotic Futures*, Tongji University Press (Shanghai), 2015, pp 66–73.
6. Fabio Gramazio and Matthias Kohler, *Digital Materiality in Architecture*, Lars Müller (Baden), 2008, pp 7–15.
7. Project 51578378 supported by the National Natural Science Foundation of China.

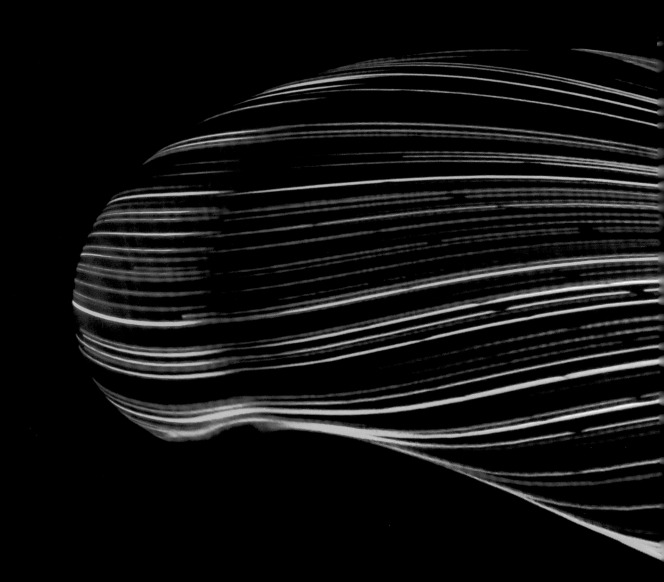

'Super-Natural'

Parametricism in Product Design

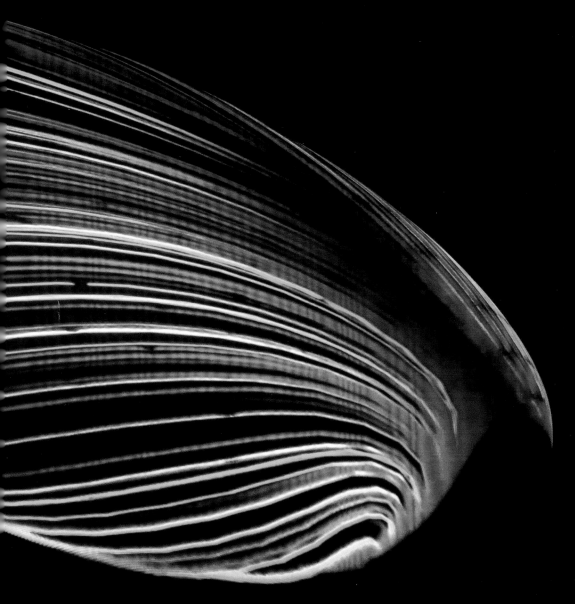

Ross Lovegrove studio,
Instinctive Override,
2013

The selection of instinct over
science to determine and arrive
at a form or design relating
specifically to human emotions,
the human subconscious and
primordial awareness:

As a stylistic movement, Parametricism has the scope to move beyond the limits of architecture, penetrating adjacent disciplines. Renowned industrial designer **Ross Lovegrove**, known as 'Captain Organic' for his nature-inspired designs, acknowledges the potential of 'new codes of creation' being incubated in architecture schools for product design, accelerating innovation across materials, structures and manufacturing technologies.

Yesterday I attended a mid-term review at the Bartlett School of Architecture here in London. It was the unit of Daniel Widrig, associate programme coordinator with Alisa Andrasek. Stepping off the street and into the otherworldliness of forms, geometries and structures that pollinate such architectural schools has an extraordinary emotional impact on one's psyche, arresting one's sense of reality of the physical environment we commonly navigate in. It is like being drawn into the wonders of a forest of beautiful botanical diversity, as if it were the missing link between what we know now and what we sense will emerge from the convergence of all things considered in the future, melded by the vast unknown capacity of the digital realm that we are immersing ourselves in.

It seems like the most natural thing in life to me, to follow an evolutionary path that harnesses the embedded logic of nature's principles in order to augment the form pool and explode the diversity of our creative potential with beauty and logic.

BEYOND KNOWN INDUSTRIAL GEOMETRIES

At the heart of this Burgess Shale moment in the discovery of new codes of creation at the genesis level are advanced schools of architecture – and not, unfortunately, schools of product design. This for me is perplexing, especially since we are in an age of enlightenment whereby the acceleration of innovation across materials, structures and technologies is profound.

Why use digital tools to create analogue forms, why 3D-print boxes or in any way replicate the past with poor uninspiring geometries, when in front of us lies a paradise of possibilities with an open agenda to break free in all dimensions? Holding it back is a troubled mind-set in design and to some degree the conflict that lies between the rational and emotional: totally understandable, as the practicalities that govern everyday universal products and their usefulness are different from the singularity of architectural construct.

Products are replicants, and we live in an age of great industrial influence over the production of food, medicines, cars, consumer electronics and clothes. The optimisation that can be achieved through scale denotes that economic and functional factors tend to drive the design of products, and it is important to note that the most successful company on Earth, APPLE Inc, at this point in time fully extrapolates and advances known production technologies and does not touch Parametricism in any way that we are currently aware of.

However, what we are discussing here is the road to the inevitable in that the absolute key to the future of it all is in the transformation of manufacturing technologies in total synergy with advances in software, artificial intelligence, materials science evolving at a nano or atomic scale, biomimetics and the alignment with the core logic of nature's economic sincerity.

Ross Lovegrove studio, Ty Nant PET bottle, 2000–2002

left: This bottle, for a brand of springwater from Bethania in Wales, was the first computer-generated universal polymer product in the world to use algorithms and non-uniform rational basis splines (NURBS) to attain high trinity in material, technology and form.

right: The first digital sketch by Ross Lovegrove, generated on a first-generation Wacom tablet as a form of digital 21st-century Impressionism.

NATURE'S ECONOMIC SINCERITY

We must remain mindful of the sincerity of economic form derived from biomorphic evolution: forms that are pure and sincere, adhering to what I call 'OE' or Organic Essentialism. This is the underlying law by which all of the products I design are initially governed in order to remain true to genesis principles that combine structure, material and minimal mass. Such objects grow through coded intrinsic forces arriving at their optimum form, arrested by extrinsic forces of natural scale and physical harmony with their condition or environment.

The DNA Staircase (2002–4) developed for my studio in composite technology demonstrates how a single module can be rotated and stacked to read as a single element forming the link between human scale and architectural volume. There is a truth and a modesty in this, and now with advanced software programs we can run sequences that project forward such principles into extremely finite and resolved entities in architectural, product, aeronautics and automotive design. The ultimate destination of such convergence will be that incredible moment in time when we will arrive at a point of optimised levels of holistic integration between form, material and function, throughout all design disciplines.

I say this because the most advanced architecture that I see today is disparately dislocated from the whole, not in the prescriptive sense but because, as structures become more and more biomorphic, they present extraordinary opportunities to create living organisms that relate more to nature's paradigms than to the old isms of architecture defined purely by aesthetics. It would be so experiential to live in a world whereby the physicality of the environment we create, from the micro to the macro, is in harmony with the natural biosphere we populate.

DIATOMIC BEAUTY AND LOGIC

The references that I have seen over the last 10 years or so in architectural and automotive schools – such as fractal theory, subdivision, biomimetics and amplification of diatomic radiolarian structures etc – have not been commonplace as study references in design. Such references, often taken as superficially aesthetic, are better applied when their base mathematical codes are understood, thus opening up a plethora of possibilities in terms of combining structure, material and finite appropriation of material volume, relating more to bioengineering than to subjective design.

DIATOM (2013–15) is a pressed aluminium chair that starts with pure geometries and then advances through the layering and refinement process that my studio practises in order to arrive at an uncompromised level of aesthetic charge and industrial logic in harmony as one. It is a recent work that uses Parametricism in order to press the surface of the aluminium with a rationalised migrant array of micro points, locally reinforcing the skin, resulting in reduced material mass and greater structural integrity without additives or substructures. This is, for me, a new principle that can relate as much to the roof of a building as to the skin of a car, the wings of an aeroplane or indeed even more commonplace everyday objects which pollinate our lives and require tactile enrichment.

Ross Lovegrove studio,
DNA Composite Staircase,
2002-4

An example of 'Organic Essentialism' using vertebrate modularity and made from fibre-reinforced plastic, Kevlar and carbon. View from below.

Ross Lovegrove studio,
DIATOM chair for Moroso,
2013-15

Pressed aluminium vertical stack chair of extreme optimisation between material, technology and geometry using parametric modelling. Data generation and modelling by Christoph Herman.

below top:
Computational model using Grasshopper to generate the sophisticated bioluminescent responsive flow-path throughout a milled, multilayered plexi tile. Data generation and modelling by Christoph Herman. head of Parametricism at Lovegrove studio.

Ross Lovegrove studio,
Twin'Z electric car for Renault France,
2012–13

below bottom:
Computational model using Grasshopper to create a driver-centric flow path and ossified lightweight seats; ultimately to expand space and holistically integrate all interior functions. Data generation and modelling by Christoph Herman.

RENAULT ADVANCED STUDY

A starting point for this exploration in my work has been the Twin'Z: a fully optimised electric car for Renault presented in Milan in 2013. Despite having to conform to the genetic coding of Renault's heritage, this small car goes some way to opening up a new seamless arterial transition from advanced contemporary software to the physical construct of highly complex, multi-material, multi-component global products. It would have advanced more biologically and thus been more purposeful not only because it was made from carbon composite but more so if it were not locked into brand communication; surely it was better to revert it towards a form that was a consequence of anatomical containment, motion and applied physics, advancing us towards a new genesis point beyond design.

We have been presented with new tools that vastly expand and amplify our ability to articulate complexity, and I feel that the relationship between products and architecture is like seeing a fantastic spaceship heading out into space, leaving those without foresight behind. Saying this of course is inflammatory to those who say that modesty is personified in a cube; but actually our own human body is so modest, and yet it is a revelation in terms of form, function and material appropriation, not to mention the magic of it running on its own fuel cells.

What Parametricism can bring to this is running sequences of diversity and accelerated mutation in order to bring to life the beauty and rarefication of the individual in the way we are and the way our deep instinctive consciousness responds to life forms. It is a way of creating what I term 'mass individualism', something fundamental to all species; and so, by reverting industry to a cell-specific model of building in the biological sense, we can run sequences that are potentially so succinct and life-enhancing. Remember that products today are constructed, but perhaps in the future they will be grown through nano-deposition.

Remember that products today are constructed, but perhaps in the future they will be grown through nano-deposition.

right:
Bioengineered wheel and tyre,
achieving material and structural transition from
its core to its traction surface.

Ross Lovegrove studio,
Twin'Z electric car for Renault France,
2012-13

below:
The real car viewed from a position above and to the rear,
showing the flow lines that migrate and animate across the
roofscape linking light-consciousness
to the driver and passenger.

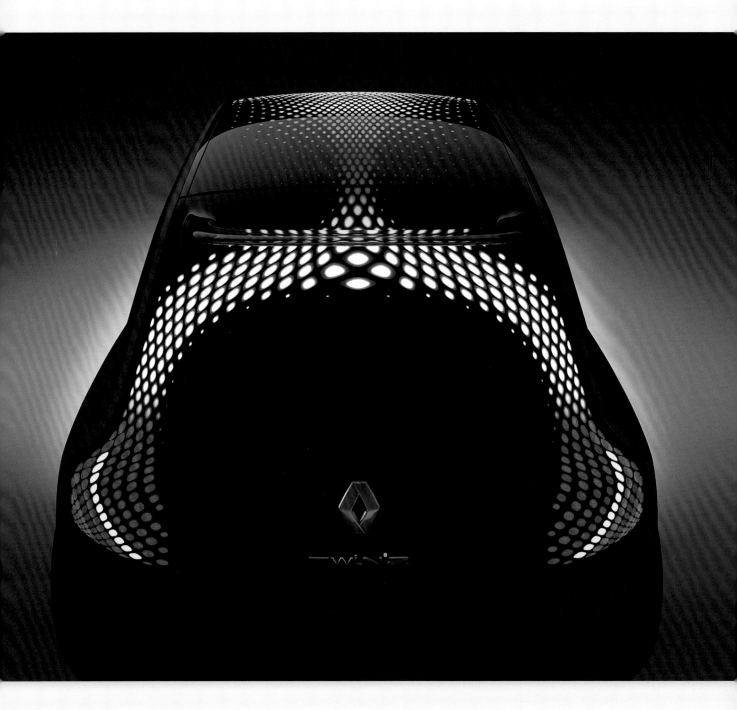

'CALGAT': CAN A LILY GROW A TELEPHONE

In the future, it is quite conceivable that products will be able to be grown biologically by agricultural methods fusing nutrients and minerals by natural cellular deposition – as suggested by my 'CALGAT' (Can a Lily Grow A Telephone) of 2010. Biomimicry will be key to this radical advance as we emulate the physicality of the natural world from the optical transparency of eyes, bioluminescence and chlorophyllic principles of solar gain to the calcification of structures and atomic-scale carbon diversity.

This is surely speculation, but what I see being embraced/released with such belief and energy in certain architectural schools by students from all cultural backgrounds is astonishing and, despite lacking current application, it is only a matter of time before its influence is more widely felt through the multiplicity of three-dimensional design.

Ross Lovegrove studio,
CALGAT (Can a Lily Grow
a Telephone),
2010

The silent growth of a cellphone out of a plant
as bio-industrialised speculation on the
future of cell growth systems into
biospherically compatible products.
Data generation and
modelling by Julia Koerner.

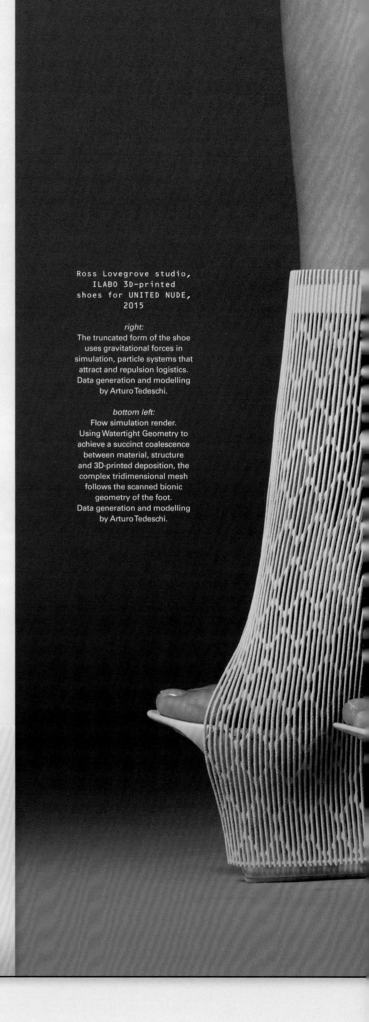

Ross Lovegrove studio,
ILABO 3D-printed
shoes for UNITED NUDE,
2015

right:
The truncated form of the shoe
uses gravitational forces in
simulation, particle systems that
attract and repulsion logistics.
Data generation and modelling
by Arturo Tedeschi.

bottom left:
Flow simulation render.
Using Watertight Geometry to
achieve a succinct coalescence
between material, structure
and 3D-printed deposition, the
complex tridimensional mesh
follows the scanned bionic
geometry of the foot.
Data generation and modelling
by Arturo Tedeschi.

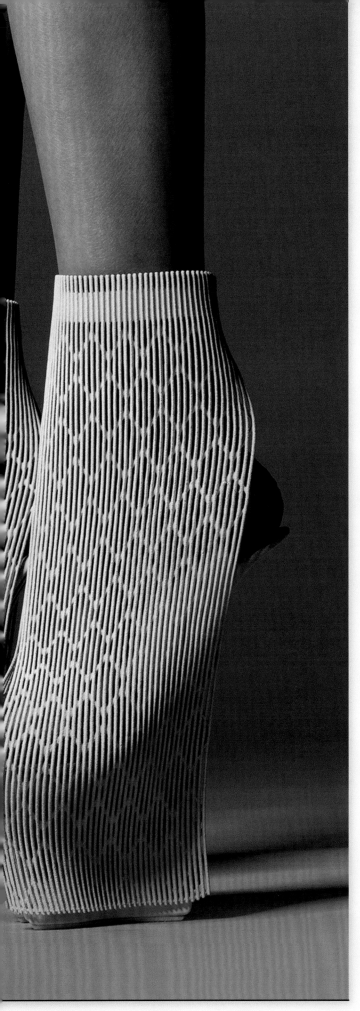

GRAVITATIONAL SHOES FOR UNITED NUDE

The shoes that I designed for UNITED NUDE in 2015 were modelled by Arturo Tedeschi, a leader in the field of McNeel Grasshopper® computational architecture. We employed attraction and repulsion logistics paralleling the bionic geometry of the foot, the data of which came from a full medical-level 3D life scan.

This project in fact polarises the convergence of design, bioengineering and architecture in the emergent field of additive manufacture. The shoes' watertight tridimensional mesh creates a visible geometry whereby nothing is extraneous either in function or material, suggesting that, if indeed form is to follow function, it can do so now in extraordinarily organic and unbridled ways that open up a new wonderland of 21st-century intelligent aesthetics.

CONVERGENCE

'In biology material is expensive but shape is cheap. As of today the opposite was true in the case of technology.'[1] This highly perceptive observation by Julian Vincent is key to understanding the potential of the way forward in creating new physical entities and stimulating a new-found value system based upon advanced convergent thinking.

As artificial intelligence evolves in unison with software and new ways of digitally being able to assimilate and run future sequences that auto-cross-reference between materials, technology, structure and purpose, we will begin to witness a new period of enlightenment whereby the physicality of the man-made environment around us will begin to grow organically as an integrated and correlated intelligent system. This organic system will embrace Parametricism as a form of evolutionary autopilot, and when we begin to design, it will act like a mother of all knowledge, diverting, mutating and testing all conceivable permutations in order to help us find the optimum solution.

So convergent theory will embrace all things considered, from multidimensional printing of all materials and compositions of materials to evolutionary growth and adaptation, along with advanced software and new technologies yet to be discovered, initiated by our fast-emerging exponential understanding of quantum physics and mechanics. Design as we now know it will be replaced with computational intelligence for mass production, leaving room for research at ground level into the idiosyncrasies that emerge from craft- and art-based human experiment. ∆

Note
1. Julian Vincent, 'Biomimetic Patterns in Architectural Design', ∆ *Patterns of Architecture*, November/December (no 6), 2009, pp 74–81.

Advancing Social Functionality Via Agent-Based Parametric Semiology

Patrik Schumacher

With the launch of Parametricism 2.0, Guest-Editor **Patrik Schumacher** asserts how Parametricism as a movement now needs to shift its main focus from computation and technological advancement towards social function. Here he advocates how Parametricism should realise its semiotic potential, with the power to express complex spatial arrangements in large-scale projects and a full spectrum of programmes for diverse users.

Parametricism presents a unique opportunity for the refounding of architectural semiology as agent-based parametric semiology. This article explores how the built environment can be designed as a system of signification that communicates its complex spatial structure and rich offering of designated spaces with diverse programmatic contents to a multitude of interrelated user groups. This re-foundation relies on a new methodology: the use of generalised crowd modelling (life-process modelling) that brings the meaning of the designed spaces – the designated functions or interaction processes – into the design model. This allows for the elaboration and successive refinement of the design with respect to its social functionality – its ultimate criteria of success in terms of the life and communication processes to be facilitated: density, diversity, relevancy and quality of interaction scenarios.

The overarching theme of this issue of $\triangle$ – the relaunching of Parametricism as Parametricism 2.0 – posits that a mature paradigm and style that has the ambition to go mainstream, to become the hegemonic epochal style of the contemporary era, must do more than merely provoke and inspire through newness and virtuoso form-making. At least some of the protagonists of Parametricism must start to explicate the style's capacities and advantages, and indeed demonstrate its superior performance in terms of both technical and social functionality.

Demonstrations of Parametricism's technical superiority are well under way in the domains of structural optimisation, adaptive environmental engineering, and CNC fabrication and robotic construction. Parametricism is indeed congenial to the new computationally empowered engineering intelligence in its methodologies as well as its rich formal repertoire and aesthetic values calling everywhere for rule-based differentiation and correlation. The design research of protagonists like Mark Burry, Achim Menges, Marc Fornes and Philippe Block demonstrates this congeniality and shows how it can lead to new technological best practice.

In fact, the architectural protagonists of Parametricism have been pushing their engineers along a new path of optimising differentiation that has exposed older forms of engineering and fabrication that were tied to the Modernist canon as irrational and wasteful. They have thus taken on the role of proto-engineers in the advancement of the technical functionality of the built environment. While this goes on (and will continue to do so in future), the attention of the movement needs to shift from technological advancement towards a long-overdue focus on the social functionality of the built environment. This is where architecture's true core competency must be located, while the technical functionality of the built environment is ultimately the responsibility of the engineering disciplines.

All Design is Communication Design

The social functionality of architecture resides to a large extent in its communicative capacity. The built environment orders social processes through its pattern of spatial separations and connections that in turn facilitates a desired pattern of separate and connected social events. This is social organisation via spatial organisation. However, it is important to reflect that the functioning of the desired social interaction scenarios depends on the participants' successful orientation and navigation within the designed environment. The built environment, with its

Zaha Hadid Architects, Galaxy Soho, Beijing 2012

opposite and below: The designed urban space is an information-rich social environment, a navigable and legible 360-degree interface of communication where interaction offerings are presented above, below and all around in layers, and where new deep vistas open up with each step forward.

complex matrix of territorial distinctions, is (or should become) a giant, navigable, information-rich interface of communication.

Before a specific interaction event can commence, relevant participants must find each other, gather and configure into a constellation that is germane to the desired interaction scenario. Their respective expectations, moods and modes of behaviour must be mutually complementary; they must share a common definition of the situation. It is therefore the spatially predefined situation that brings all actors on to the same page, and into a conducive position, with their respective, compatible and/or complementary social roles. The built environment thus delivers a necessary precondition of determinate social interaction. (This is indeed the profound societal function of the built environment and the specific responsibility of the discipline of architecture and urban design.)

In order for this to succeed, the built environment must be legible to the prospective participants. This legibility has both a phenomenological and a semiological aspect. The phenomenological aspect requires that each participant is able to perceptually decompose the spatio-visual field into identifiable units of interaction as a precondition of his or her orientation. The semiological aspect requires further that each participant understands the social meaning of the spatial units he or she can identify within the environment. The participant can then respond to the spatial communication that is broadcast by the designed space, for example by entering the space or social situation.

As a communicative frame, a designed space is itself a premise for all communications that take place within its boundaries. Designed spaces deliver the necessary predefinition of the respective designated social situation, thereby reducing the otherwise unmanageable excess of possible actions that exist in our complex contemporary societies. They 'frame' social interaction. Spatial communication/framing is thus architecture's core competency. It implies that the built environment can be understood as a text or permanent broadcast that represents and informs us about the social order we must navigate and participate in. All social institutions that involve the interaction of simultaneously or successively present participants rely on architecture's framing communicative capacity, and thus on its semiological or semantic dimension. The elaboration of spatial complexes as systems of signification is therefore promoted here as a key to upgrading architecture's core competency.

The Re-foundation of Architectural Semiology

The semantic dimension of architecture is a crucial aspect of its ordering function. That all architecture and urbanism has an inevitable semantic dimension is generally accepted. However, so far nobody seems to have succeeded in making this an arena of explicit, strategic design effort. Earlier attempts to develop an architectural semiology (under the auspices of Postmodernism) failed to convince.[1] There was too much reliance on familiar motifs, which hampered innovation. More importantly, the task was not clearly delimited, and no means to operationalise the concept of meaning was available. Consequently, not much was achieved and the whole idea was rejected in the early 1990s when 'performance' was counterposed to 'representation'. This opposition was the expression of a necessary retreat from an unproductive engagement with semiology. However, such opposition is false, and the correct formula is: 'performance via representation'. Architecture functions via its semantic associations as much as it does so via physical separation and connection. The built environment functions through its visual appearance, legibility and related capacity to frame and prime communication. It is not just channelling bodies, but orienting sentient, socialised beings who must actively comprehend and navigate ever more complex urban scenes.

The distinction between the technical functioning of the built environment and its social functioning was outlined above. While technical functioning considers the physical integrity, constructability and physical performance of the building in relation to its users understood as physical-biological bodies, architecture must also take into consideration a building's social function as an ordering and guiding communicative frame that succeeds via its visual legibility. The core competency of architecture is thus the task of articulation. Legibility involves two aspects: perceptual tractability/palpability and retrievability of semantic-informational content. Accordingly, architectural theory distinguishes phenomenological articulation and semiological articulation.

The relationship between the technical and the articulatory dimension of the built environment leads to the concept of tectonics, here understood as the architectural selection and utilisation of initially technically motivated, engineered forms and details for the sake of a legible articulation that aims at an information-rich, communicative spatial morphology.

Alessandro Boccacci and Mark Eichler, Google Campus, Parametric Semiology design studio (tutors: Patrik Schumacher and Marc Fornes), Harvard University Graduate School of Design (GSD), Cambridge, Massachusetts, 2013

Tectonics is the utilisation of technically indicated morphologies for the purposes of communicative articulation. The complex variegated order proposed within contemporary architecture is reflected and accentuated by optimised, adaptive structures.

Entering a territory implies an acceptance of its spatial communication, and thus communicates one's willingness to participate in the respective interaction scenario.

Every designer adapts to and intervenes intuitively within the spontaneous and historically evolving semiological system of the built environment. The aim of architectural semiology research is to move from an intuitive participation within an evolving semiosis to an explicit agenda that understands the design of a large-scale architectural complex as an opportunity to create a new, coherent system of signification, a new (artificial) architectural language, without relying on the familiar codes found in existing built environments.

An important premise of the refounding of architectural semiology is the necessity to limit the domain of the signified: architecture does not symbolise everything and it does not tell us stories; it must only tell us what to expect within its bounds (or in its vicinity). We need to ask: What does the user need to know about an urban or architectural environment, and what can an urban or architectural space communicate about itself? The answer is threefold: we expect a space to communicate its designated function, then who the space belongs to, and finally what we might expect to find beyond our current field of vision. The three dimensions to which we must limit the domain of the signified of any architectural language can thus be defined as 'function type', 'social type' and 'location type'. This restriction is both necessary and empowering. The failure to delimit the domain of the signified was one of the reasons why the earlier Postmodernist semiology could not succeed.

The next preliminary clarification concerns the minimal unit of any meaningful architectural sign or communication. In verbal language it is the sentence that constitutes the minimal unit of communication. In any prospective architectural language only a spatially defined territory can function as such a complete sign or minimal unit of meaning. Architectural elements or motifs can only count as incomplete sign radicals that by themselves communicate nothing, but might contribute to the demarcation and characterisation of a territory or place. The crossing of a demarcation or threshold implies the entering of a different place and different (potential) social situation. The spatial distinction implies a social distinction. Only a territory is a full communication; that is, something that calls for being either accepted or rejected.

Each territory is a communication. It communicates an invitation to participate in the framed social situation. Entering a territory implies an acceptance of its spatial communication, and thus communicates one's willingness to participate in the respective interaction scenario. Everybody who enters is expected to adopt the behavioural rules implied. (That is the point of all signification: the coordination of behaviours facilitating cooperation.) The precise characterisation of the situation depends upon the orchestration of the various semiological registers that come together in the articulated territory: its position in the overall matrix of territories, its spatial shape, tectonic and material articulation and so on. The articulate territory might thus be designed according to a 'grammar' as a well-formed combination of sign radicals. The build-up of a spatio-visual grammar affords a momentous combinatorial enhancement of architecture's versatility of expression. A small vocabulary might afford a vast number of different communications.[2]

The re-foundation of architectural semiology presented here is thus based on three premises, or axioms: (1) the domain of the signified is limited to function type, social type and location type; (2) the territory is the minimal unit of signification/communication; and (3) architectural semiology must exploit the combinatorial power of grammar. However, although these important innovations make semiology in architecture viable, the most important innovation of architectural semiology's re-foundation as agent-based parametric semiology is the introduction of crowd modelling as a crucial device to represent the meanings of the designed architectural communications

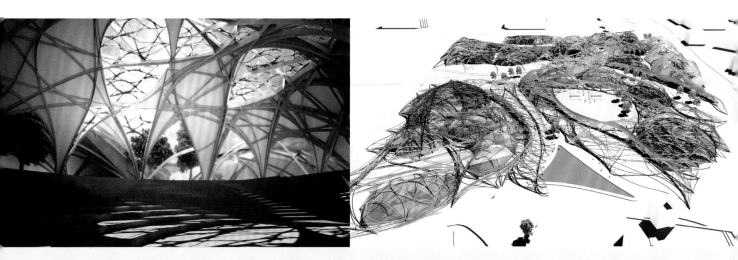

Felix Luong, John Morrison and Joseph Ross, Google Campus, Parametric Semiology design studio (tutors: Patrik Schumacher and Marc Fornes), Harvard University Graduate School of Design (GSD), Cambridge, Massachusetts, 2013

A project like Google Campus is a pertinent vehicle to speculate on the productivity of interconnected and inter-aware spaces for dynamic, intensely networked patterns of communication. The convex curvature of the shells makes the spatial units and relations easily recognisable and traceable even if the units proliferate and interpenetrate in complex arrangements.

within the design model. This thus leads to a fourth axiom: (4) the signified is integrated into the design model via agent-based life-process modelling. This novel methodology delivers a potent operationalisation of semiology within architecture.

Operationalisation Via Agent-Based Life-Process Modelling

The functional heuristics of Parametricism understand the functions of spaces in terms of dynamic patterns of social communication; that is, as parametrically variable, dynamic event scenarios rather than in terms of static schedules of accommodation that list functional stereotypes. It has now become possible to model the thus understood functional layer of the city and incorporate it within an iterative design process using computational crowd-simulation techniques and agent-based models. Such models reproduce and predict collective patterns of movement, occupation and interaction as emerging from individual rule-based actions.

The social-functional layer of architecture – according to the appropriate delimitation of the domain of the signified – is at the same time its semantic layer, and both can now be worked on via agent-based crowd modelling. It is of great importance that architectural semiology can hook its ambitions onto a new design simulation tool that is bound to become a pervasive medium to test and anticipate architecture's social functionality. The augmentation of design projects by means of agent-based crowd modelling enables us to test and ascertain the enhancement of the design's social functionality; gains in operational efficiency delivered by the semiologically augmented design should become manifest via the crowd simulation. This ambitious agenda will in turn leave its innovative imprint on the very premises and tools of

crowd simulation. Three key innovations are on the horizon: the generalisation of crowd modelling from circulation flow simulations to a generalised life-process modelling; the shift from physically conceived to communicatively conceived agents with the crucial augmentation of sign- or frame-dependent behaviours; and the differentiation of agents according to different social roles.

Frame dependency is a crucial aspect of the generalisation of crowd modelling. Only in circulation scenarios (and especially in evacuation scenarios that reduce the problem to physical bottlenecks) can the simulation abstract from the encoded social meanings that otherwise always structure and modulate behaviour. As soon as we move beyond these exceptional scenarios to the simulation of interaction scenarios – such as a gallery opening event – we must indeed augment our agents with a semiological capacity to deliver social sensitivity, where their behaviours are regulated by an assumed or designed system of signification.

The modulation of the agent's behavioural rules is made dependent on the configurational and morphological features of the environment designed in accordance with a semiological code. Agents must thus be implemented with a whole stack of different behavioural scripts, while the crossing of spatial thresholds triggers behavioural script switches or modulations. This indeed initiates a crucial innovation within the field of crowd modelling.[3] Only on the basis of such frame dependency can we move from the current evacuation- and traffic-engineering crowds to architectural and semiological crowds as the basis for generalised life-process simulation. The framing environments must be designed accordingly as systems of signification that encode the diversity of behavioural scripts.

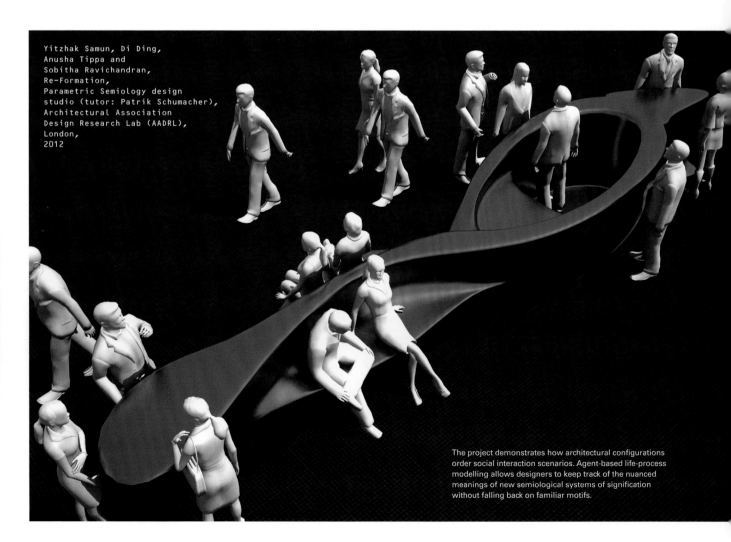

Yitzhak Samun, Di Ding,
Anusha Tippa and
Sobitha Ravichandran,
Re-Formation,
Parametric Semiology design
studio (tutor: Patrik Schumacher),
Architectural Association
Design Research Lab (AADRL),
London,
2012

The project demonstrates how architectural configurations order social interaction scenarios. Agent-based life-process modelling allows designers to keep track of the nuanced meanings of new semiological systems of signification without falling back on familiar motifs.

A designed system of signification works if the programmed social agents consistently respond to the relevant coded positional and morphological clues so that the expected behaviours can in turn be read off the articulated environmental configuration. What is important to appreciate here is that the global event pattern – for example, the successful mingling pattern at the gallery opening – must be constituted from the bottom up by autonomous individual agents who act on the basis of their frame-dependent behavioural scripts. This operates according to the dialectic of simple individual/local rules and (potentially complex) emergent global/collective patterns.

The meaning of architecture – the prospective life processes it frames and sustains – is modelled and assessed within architecture's design process, thus becoming a direct object of creative speculation and cumulative design elaboration. This allows for the iterative refinement of the design with respect to its ultimate criteria of success in terms of the life and communication processes to be facilitated: footfall, dwelling time, encounter frequency and diversity, quality of interaction scenarios and so on.

Enhancing Architecture's Communicative Capacity

This article has presented a new key working methodology that focuses on architecture's core competency. It thus seems reasonable to expect that the generalised life-process modelling envisioned here should become compelling to both architects and clients as a new standard for best practice in architecture. Then a drawing or model that does not include crowds or agents can no longer count as an architectural drawing or model. The presence of crowds/agents within the model thus becomes the demarcation criterion that identifies and distinguishes architecture and design from the engineering disciplines.

The augmentation of spatial organisation with semiological articulation should lead to a decisive augmentation of architecture's comunicative capacity, and thus its ability to deliver an enhanced social functionality. A semiologically cohered, information-rich environment gives every user more intuitively retrievable information and awareness. Further, rule-based parametric design establishes chains of dependency (correlations) that deliver legible inference potentials[4] from what is seen to what is not yet seen, in all three dimensions of the domain of the signified: function type, social type and location type.

We can no longer assume the users' familiarity with specific localities. Instead we need to rely more on a general language of space, within each large project (such as a corporate campus) or indeed from project to project. A new Google campus, for example, is a relevant design task that would benefit from the design methodology proposed here. Such a campus should be designed as a richly differentiated system of signification, and tested by agent simulations that can begin to demonstrate that users' utilisation of the enhanced information-richness of the designed environment leads to a life process of superior productivity according to relevant measures like space utilisation, navigation efficiency, the smooth flow of activities, encounter frequency and relevancy, interaction density, variety and duration. These criteria of success would indicate the comparative enhancement of the life process in terms of the overall desired outcome: work satisfaction, learning and productivity. ⌀

Agent-based life-process modelling allows designers to speculate about the social meaning of unusual architectural forms. Here, a lecture theatre morphs gradually into a lounging area.

Notes
1. See Charles Jencks and George Baird (eds), *Meaning in Architecture*, George Braziller (New York), 1970.
2. For a more detailed account see Patrik Schumacher, 'The Semiological Project and the General Project of Architectural Order', *The Autopoiesis of Architecture, Vol II: A New Agenda for Architecture*, John Wiley & Sons (Chichester), 2012, pp 238–50.
3. The author is currently collaborating with BuroHappold's Smart Space dedicated crowd-modelling team to implement the idea of frame-dependent semiological crowds. This innovation is a necessary consequence of generalising crowd simulations beyond those of circulation to encompass all human activities and modes of interaction in their dependency on designated spaces and spatial contexts.
4. If A determines B, then B indicates A.

Hegemonic Parametricism Delivers a Market-Based Urban Order

Patrik Schumacher

London is a paradigmatic
exemplar of the urban
concentration process in global
hub cities. As more and more
large iconic structures pile into
the financial district, the urban
landscape becomes more and
more chaotic, an unintentional
bricolage. The planning process
is evidently failing to stem
the visual chaos and unable
to establish any semblance of
urban order.

How might Parametricism be
widely adopted at an urban scale?
Guest-Editor **Patrik Schumacher**
argues that Parametricism 2.0
has now matured sufficiently
at a technical and stylistic level
to engage with the creation of
'a complex, variegated urban
order'. Moreover, he avows that it
should be adequately adaptable
to respond to the dynamic forces
influencing global markets,
assuming a prominent position
as a mainstream movement.

Parametricism 2.0 makes urbanism and urban order
compatible with the neo-liberal re-emergence of market
processes after the demise of Modernism – the golden era
of urbanism. Large-scale city planning receded during the
1980s, and since then urbanism as a discourse, discipline
and profession has all but disappeared. This coincided with
the crisis of Modernism, which had begun in the 1970s,
and can be interpreted as the way in which the demise
of the Fordist planned economy manifested itself within
architecture. The bankruptcy of Modernist urban planning
gave way everywhere to the same visual chaos of laissez-faire
urban expansion under the auspices of stylistic pluralism
and the anti-method of collage. However, in the last 15
years, innovative urbanism re-emerged under the banner
of 'Parametric Urbanism',[1] developing the conceptual,
formal and computational resources for forging a complex,
variegated urban order on the basis of parametric logics
that allow it to adapt to dynamic market forces. The global
convergence and maturation of Parametricist design research
implies that this style of urbanism is ready to go mainstream
and impact the global built environment by re-establishing
strong urban identities on the basis of its adaptive and
evolutionary heuristics.

The Historical Task of Urban Intensification
Since the 1980s we have witnessed a sustained drive towards
urban concentration in global hub cities. Within contemporary
network society, the productivity of everybody depends on
being plugged into urban professional and cultural networks
that exist only in the big cities. What each of us is doing
needs to be continuously recalibrated with what everybody
else is doing. All further productivity gains depend on this,
and it requires a new level of communicative density that
is only available in the metropolis. This underlies what

economists measure as 'agglomeration economies'. In the
provinces, entrepreneurs and workers are cut off and thus
relatively unproductive. Since the neat division into work
and leisure has disappeared and we feel the vital urge to
remain connected to the network 24/7, it is as important for
us to live in the city as it is inevitable for us to work in it.
Everything piles into the centre, the more the better. This
spells a new desire for an unprecedented degree of urban
intensification.

London, with its relentless growth (and yet endemic
undersupply of accommodation) is a paradigmatic
exemplar of the urban concentration process in global
hub cities. This new urban dynamic is a fascinating
challenge for architects, but more degrees of freedom are
first required that enable urban entrepreneurs (and their
architects) to experiment, discover and create the best
ways to weave this urban texture and garner potential
synergies through innovative intricate programmatic
juxtapositions. Only an unhampered market process can
offer the freedom and incentives required to discover and
implement the productive synergies that allow our cities
to thrive. Only markets have the information processing
capacity and agility to assemble a viable complex urban
order for this novel societal context.[2] This is why positive,
physical Modernist urban planning had to be abandoned,
and planning thereafter was confined to operating
negatively, by means of restricting private actors. The
result is a less regulated form of urbanisation. This mode
of development is certainly better adapted to the new
socioeconomic processes than the bankrupt, simplistic
order of Modernist planning and urbanism. However,
it produces an urban scene that is perceptually hard to
digest, a paradoxical and menacing phenomenological
sameness despite the rich diversity of its contents.

Garbage Spill Urbanisation

While the new diversity and open-endedness of post-Fordist social phenomena is being accommodated, the unregulated agglomeration of differences has produced the global effect of white-noise sameness everywhere, without allowing for the emergence of distinct urban identities. The result is a disorienting visual chaos that might best be termed 'garbage spill urbanisation'. Like in a garbage spill, the urban agglomeration's diversity of ingredients is no longer perceptually decipherable. Tokyo is perhaps the most notorious (and often celebrated) example of visual urban chaos that spells both vitality and menacing disorientation. There is indeed an underlying, market-driven programmatic order, due to the market participants' persistent hunt for synergies. However, due to an over-abundance of material construction possibilities and attendant stylistic choices, this order is rendered obscure.

This phenomenological disarticulation of the city's organisational complexity hampers the full potential for complex social ordering because it compromises the vital communicative capacity of the built environment. Social functionality depends as much on subjective visual accessibility as it does on objective physical availability. Social cooperation requires that specifically relevant actors find each other and configure within specific communicative situations. The failure to grasp this instrumentality of the built environment's appearance has for too long hindered architecture's proactive pursuit of formal articulation as a key competency of the discipline.[3]

This insight motivates the attempt to articulate a complex variegated urban order that allows for intuitive navigation and orientation within an information-rich built environment that makes its offerings visually accessible; that is, the design agenda of Parametricism and parametric urbanism.

There is no doubt that new computational ordering devices such as gradients, vector fields, and methods of associative modelling and geometric data-field transcoding allow designers to generate intricately ordered urban morphologies with distinct identities that could in principle make a much larger amount of programmatic information perceptually tractable. However, this raises the question of how this desired increase in urban order can be implemented in the face of a receding state planning apparatus.

A celebrated paradigm of urban chaos: Tokyo, 2008

top: Market-based urbanisation produces a disorienting urban disarticulation. The random agglomeration of architectural forms produces a white-noise sameness and prevents the emergence of a legible urban order and identity. Without rules of correlation there can be no inferences drawn from what is seen to what is not yet seen.

Garbage spill: all differences collapse into sameness

bottom: Garbage looks the same everywhere around the world, despite all the local differences in ingredients. A perfect analogy that explains why all urbanisation processes since the collapse of Modernism have resulted in 'ugly' environments without identity.

Like all urban agglomerations,
London expands without
bounds and without shape. The
only characteristics that give
otherwise amorphous megacities
a recognisable shape are natural
landscape features such as rivers,
hills and valleys.

Given that the various subsystems
and features within a natural
environment are correlated
through their codependent laws of
morphogenesis, they potentially
become representations of each
other, allowing one to be inferred
from the other: a legible order and
pertinent paradigm for what our
built environments should deliver.

The rule-based generation of
urban morphologies on the
basis of scripts that differentiate,
modulate and correlate the
different subsystems like fabric
fields, path systems and open
spaces delivers a complex
variegated urban order that is as
information rich and navigable as
natural landscape formations.

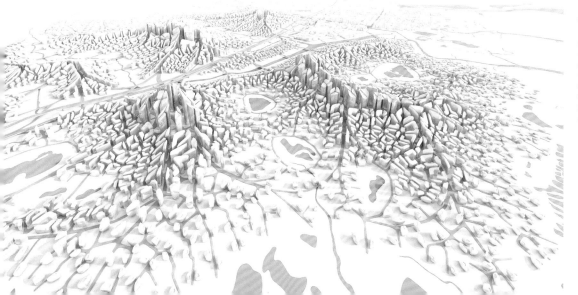

Hegemonic Parametricism Evolves a Multi-Author Urban Order

One obvious way in which the vacuum left by state planning can be filled is by means of 'private planning', a process whereby private development corporations or consortiums unify larger development areas within a coherent, market-controlled urban business strategy. Although isolated insertions continue, there is a tendency to try to merge and integrate developable land parcels within historical centres, and also towards larger and larger privately masterplanned development sites in the wider expanse of the global megacities where development is concentrated. In this sense, private planning is on the rise and thus affords opportunities for visual as much as programmatic integration. The example of London's great estates offers an encouraging historical precedent here – of private, market-based, long-term urban asset management and planning establishing an urban order that is inclusive of a visual architectural order. However, the question remains: is the degree of order that parametric urbanism aspires to possible beyond the level of integration achievable via private planning? More generally, is urbanism at all possible in the face of market-based dynamism?

The market process is an evolutionary one that operates via mutation (trial and error), selection (via profit versus loss) and reproduction (via imitation). It is self-correcting and self-regulating, leading to a self-organised order. We might therefore presume that the land-use and thus the programmatic dimension of the urban and architectural order is to be determined by architecture's private clients within a market process that allocates land resources to the most valued uses. However, in the absence of stylistic and methodological coherence we cannot expect the underlying programmatic order to become legible as a spatio-morphological one. For this to happen we must presume a hegemonic stylistic and methodological paradigm that has the versatility and ordering capacity to translate the social order into a complex variegated spatial order. A shared paradigm offers the prospect of coherence across multiple authors working for multiple clients. No controlling hand needs to be presupposed.

Parametricism can thus draw from and exploit the powerful analogy of unplanned, multi-author parametric urbanism within a multi-species ecology. Consider the way that various features and creatures within a natural environment coalesce to create a complex variegated

Studio Hadid/Schumacher,
Complex variegated order via multi-author coherence,
Istanbul Cultural District,
Yale University,
New Haven, Connecticut,
2013

This design experiment in unplanned multi-author urban order demonstrates how coherence, interarticulation and resonance can emerge if independent authors work within the shared paradigm of Parametricism that enables and calls for mutually adaptive and affiliative design moves.

order based on rules – in turn based on the complex interaction of multiple laws of nature – that establish systematic correlations between the different organic and inorganic subsystems that make up a natural landscape. The topography correlates with the path of the river; the river, together with the topography and sun orientation, differentiates the flora; and the differentiation of the flora – with the river and topography – shapes the differentiation and distribution of the fauna, which in turn impacts back on the flora and thus often also on rivers and even the topography. While this causality is complex and not easy to unravel, correlations are being established in all directions, providing information for those who want to navigate such a landscape.

The key here is the build-up of correlations and associations, irrespective of the underlying causality. Each new species of plant or animal proliferates according to its own rules of adaptation and survival. For instance, moss grows differentially on the terraced rock surfaces of certain shaded slopes depending on surface pattern, sun orientation, rock formation and so on. A population of a certain species of birds might then settle on these slopes. In the same way, Parametricism envisions the build-up of a densely layered urban environment via differentiated, rule-based architectural interventions that are designed via scripts that form new architectural subsystems, just like a new species settles into a natural environment. This process delivers rich yet fully correlated diversity if designed according to the heuristics of Parametricism. Each new architect/author can be uniquely creative in inventing and designing the rules/scripts of their own project, and participate in their own unique way in the build-up of a variegated, information-rich urban order. This analogy also extends to the navigation of rule-based environments: the urbanite's intuitive orientation within a parametric urban environment functions analogous to animal cognition/navigation in a natural environment.

Progression of Styles

Patrik Schumacher,
Progression of
Styles: Freedom vs
Order,
2015

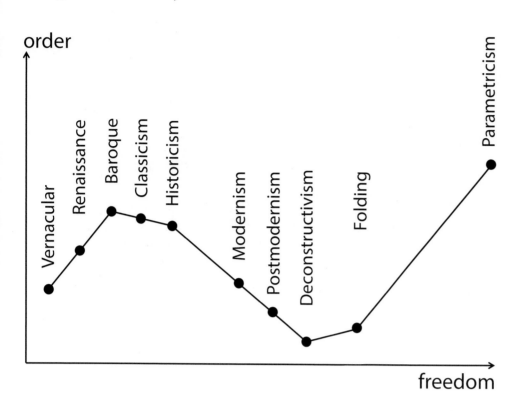

order

Vernacular · Renaissance · Baroque · Classicism · Historicism · Modernism · Postmodernism · Deconstructivism · Folding · Parametricism

freedom

Parametricism achieves an inversion of architecture's entropy law. Freedom had to be bought by giving up order until the techniques of Parametricism started to give a new, powerful ordering capacity to the discipline of architecture, one that delivers a simultaneous enhancement of freedom and order.

The Reversal of Architecture's Historical Entropy Law

Parametricism is the only viable candidate for the next hegemonic epochal style. Neither a hegemonic Postmodernism nor a hegemonic Deconstructivism could overcome the visual chaos that allows the proliferation of differences to collapse into global sameness (white noise). Both Postmodernism and Deconstructivism operate via collage, via the unconstrained agglomeration of differences. Deconstructivism can thus be seen as the aesthetic sublimation of the urban process of 'garbage spill' collage. Only Parametricism has the capacity to combine an increase in complexity with a simultaneous increase in order, via the principles of rule-based differentiation and multi-system correlation. Only Parametricism can overcome the visual chaos and white-noise sameness that laissez-faire urbanisation produces everywhere, by holding out the possibility of a market-based urbanism that produces an emergent order and local identity in a bottom-up process, without relying on political or bureaucratic power. Starting with given natural features and settlements, its values and methodological principles can produce path-dependent, self-amplifying local identities. Its ethos of contextual affiliation and ambition to establish or reinforce continuities allows for the development of unique urban identities on the basis of local contexts, topography, climate and culture.

Parametricist order does not rely on the uniform repetition of patterns as Modernist urbanism does. In contrast to

Baroque or Beaux-Arts masterplans, its compositions are inherently open ended (incomplete). Their order is relational rather than geometric. They establish order and orientation via the lawful differentiation of fields, via vectors of transformation, as well as via contextual affiliations and subsystem correlations. This requires neither the completion of a figure, nor – in contrast to Modernist masterplans – the uniform repetition of a pattern. There are always many (in principle infinitely many) creative ways to transform, to affiliate, to correlate. A unique, unpredictable, but recognisable and legible order (which allows for orienting inferences from what is seen to what is not yet seen) will emerge as long as all architects acquire the skills necessary and design within the Parametricist paradigm and ethos that calls for continuities and affiliations under the critical eye and peer pressure of each other. A hegemonic Parametricism thus offers the prospect of a market-based urban order.

If we look at the historical progression of styles, we find that the last 300 years established what might be called architecture's entropy law: all gains in terms of design freedom and versatility have been achieved at the expense of urban and architectural order. In other words, increases in versatility had to be bought by a progressive degeneration of architecture's ordering capacity. Increases in designers' degree of freedom were established via the enrichment of architecture's formal-compositional repertoire, and were a paramount criterion of progress in its pursuit of matching

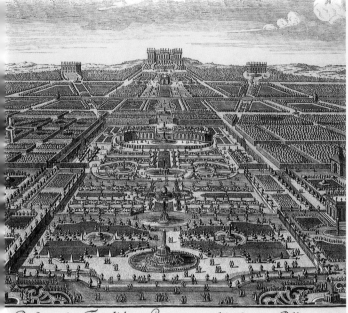

Proſpect des Fürſtlichen Luſtgartens, hinter dem Pallaſt.
Cum Privileg. Sac. Cæs. Majest.   Jeremias Wolff excud. Aug. Vind.   Ienas Heinric.

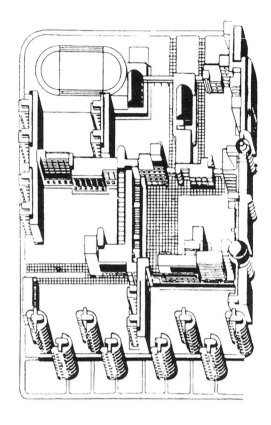

Classicism: high levels of order
– limited degrees of freedom. From
Paulus Decker, *Architectura Civilis*,
1711

top left: The ordering principles of symmetry and
proportion gave classical architecture the capacity
to compose potent unities by ordering the city
around the institutional ensemble of church and
palace.

Modernism: increased degrees of
freedom – lower levels of order.
Nicolai Kusmin, Residential Complex
for Miners, Anshero–Sudshensk,
Russia, 1930

top right: Modernism let go of the constraints of
symmetry and proportion and gained the freedom
of radical abstraction. It maintained orthogonality
and worked with the ordering principles of
separation, specialisation and limitless repetition.

Postmodernism: further increases in
degrees of freedom – further loss of
order. Madelon Vriesendorp, *The City
of the Captive Globe*, Delirious New
York, 1972

opposite: Postmodernism rejected the monotony
of Modernist separation and repetition and opened
itself up for an unconstrained juxtaposition and
collage of architectural forms and motifs from all
other periods of architecture.

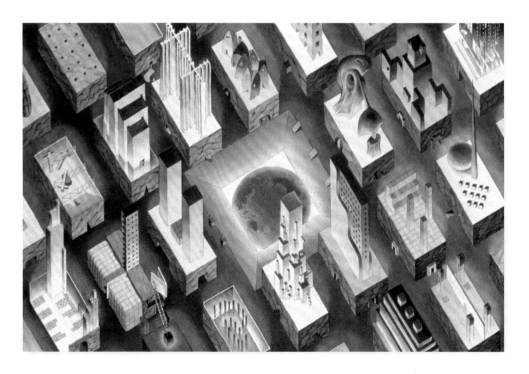

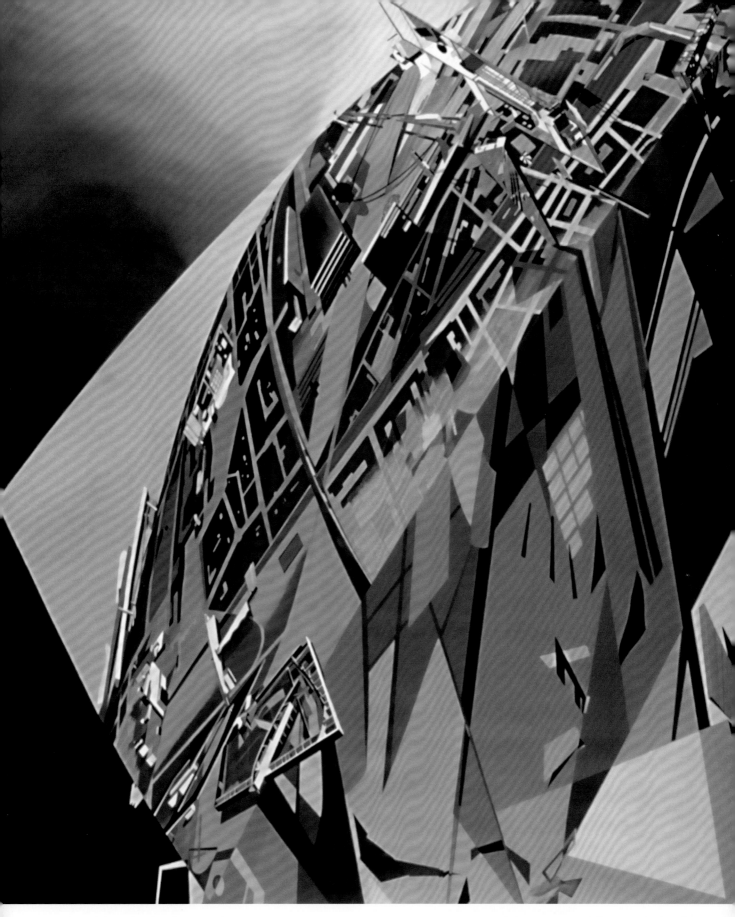

above: Deconstructivism abandoned orthogonality and
all historical motifs to regain the freedom of abstraction,
and intensified the principle of collage by allowing
superimposition and interpenetration as much as
juxtaposition.

opposite: Parametricism expands architects' repertoire and thus freedom
through spline/NURBS-based curvilinearity as well as gradient swarm
formations. It has hugely increased architecture's ordering capacity via the
scripting or agent-based emergence of associative logics.

the requisite variety of societal complexity. Like the move from Classical architecture to Modernism, the move from Modernism via Postmodernism to Deconstructivism delivered an expansion of degrees of freedom and versatility (to accommodate a more complex society) that was paid for by a relaxation or rejection of the rules of composition – of means of ordering – and thus a resultant degeneration of the visual order.

Order was progressively eroded. However, this long trend of the negative correlation of freedom and order can be reversed under the auspices of Parametricism. Parametricism offers a simultaneous increase in freedom and order and thus inaugurates a new phase of architectural negentropy. Its radical ontological and methodological innovation translates into a massive leap in both dimensions of architectural progress considered here; it entails an unprecedented expansion of architecture's compositional freedom and ordering capacity through the deployment of algorithms and via new compositional rules such as affiliations, gradients and associative logics. In principle all design moves are now rule based, and thus have the potential to enhance the visual order and legibility of the built environment in the face of increased complexity.

Parametricism is manifestly superior to all other architectural styles still pandered and pursued. This implies that it should sweep the market and put an end to the current pluralism that resulted from the crisis of Modernism, and that has been going on for far too long due to ideological inertia. This plurality of styles must make way for a universal – hegemonic – Parametricism that allows architecture to once more have a vital, decisive, transformative impact on the built environment, just as Modernism had done in the 20th century. ●

Notes
1. 'Parametric Urbanism' was the title of a three-year design research agenda at the Architectural Association Design Research Lab (AADRL) in London from 2005 to 2008.
2. It was Friedrich von Hayek who first understood economic competition to be a discovery process, and the economic problem of efficient resource allocation as that of knowledge utilisation and information processing. See Friedrich von Hayek, 'The Use of Knowledge in Society', *American Economic Review*, XXXV (4), 1945, pp 519–30, and Friedrich von Hayek, 'Competition as a Discovery Procedure', 1968, reprinted in *The Quarterly Journal of Austrian Economics*, 5 (3), Fall 2002, pp 9–23.
3. The crucial work on formal/aesthetic problems that in practice takes up the larger part of the architect's design work is being denigrated or denied in the discipline's self-descriptions. Architecture is responsible for the built environment's social (rather than technical engineering) functionality. Social functionality of the built environment depends now more and more upon its communicative capacity, which in turn is a matter of visual communication.

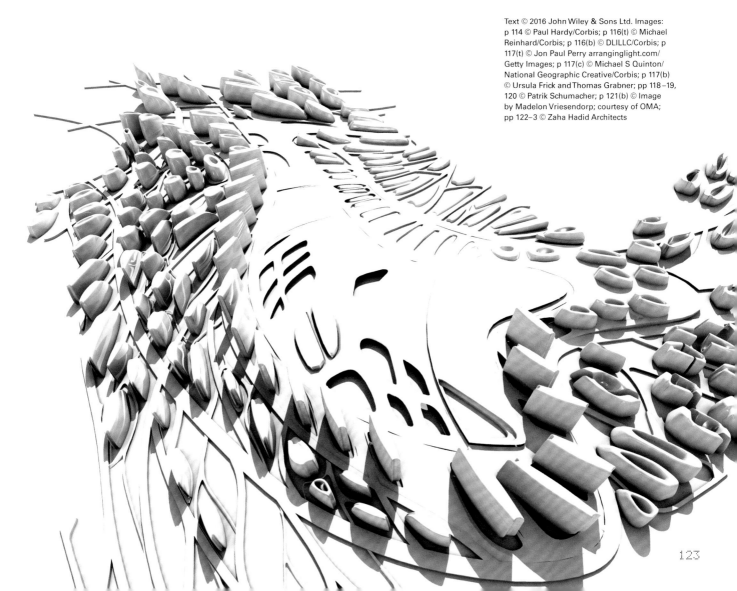

Manuel DeLanda

PARAMETRISING THE SOCIAL

As espoused by Guest-editor Patrik Schumancher, the social function of architecture is at the core of the reformulation of Parametricism 2.0. Artist and philosopher **Manuel DeLanda**, who is Professor of Graduate Architecture and Urban Design (GAUD) at Pratt Institute in New York, argues for an innovative new approach to social processes that is compatible with Parametricism. He highlights the significance of the meso-scale as a parameter; these are communities and organisations that operate between the micro-scale of the individual and the macro-scale of society as a whole.

The traditional approaches to the study of social processes take either a micro or a macro perspective. There is, of course, classical microeconomics focusing on the individual and his or her rational decisions, as well as macro-sociology in which the target of research is society as a whole. In the 20th century, economics acquired a macro approach, studying the overall rate of unemployment and inflation of a country, as well as its gross national product, while sociology developed a micro branch that investigated the socially constructed phenomenological experience of individuals. But in addition to the micro and macro scales, there is the much less well-known meso-scale, comprising social phenomena of intermediate scale: communities, institutional organisations, industrial networks, social justice movements, governments, cities and urban regions. This list is only partial, but it vividly displays the problem with traditional approaches. A large number of important social entities are left out of their domain.

Two obstacles must be removed to open the way for research on the meso-scale. The first is reductionism. If everything social can be reduced to the lives of individuals, to their decisions and their experiences, then any social entity larger than that will be inevitably neglected. The antidote to reductionism is the concept of an emergent property, a property of a whole that is caused by the interactions among its parts. If communities or organisations are conceived as entities that have properties of their own, then the temptation to reduce them to their members goes away. The other obstacle is holism, the idea that in order to prevent reductionism the existence of a seamless totality must be postulated: wholes in which relations determine the very identity of what is related (relations of interiority).

Historically, the concept of 'society as a whole' has been treated in terms of such seamless totalities. The antidote in this case is to assemble a whole using only relations of exteriority, relations that respect the relative autonomy of what is related.[1] Used together, the two concepts of emergence and exteriority permit us to conceive of wholes that are both irreducible and decomposable. Moreover, by making emergence recursive, so that an emergent whole can become a working part of a larger emergent whole, we can generate all the intermediate layers between individuals and their countries: communities can become parts of social justice movements through alliances or coalitions, and organisations become part of industrial networks through relations of resource dependency.

Wholes that are both irreducible and decomposable are referred to as assemblages. Let us illustrate the concept with some elementary examples. A tightly knit community, such as those we find in small towns or in ethnic neighbourhoods in large cities, is characterised by the fact that every community member knows every other member. When everyone knows everyone else, word of mouth travels fast, particularly when the content of the gossip is about the violation of a local norm: an unkept promise; an unreciprocated favour; an unpaid bet; a lie. Because of this, the community as a whole can be said to store the reputations of its members. In addition, when a member with a deteriorating reputation fails to mend his or her ways, the community can nformally punish him or her through ridicule and ostracism. In other words, the community can enforce local norms.

These two abilities, reputation-storage and norm-enforcement, belong to the entire assemblage, not to its parts. On the other hand, they emerge from the interactions between the parts, so they depend on the day-to-day practices of the neighbours: if the latter stop communicating or stop caring about local norms, the abilities disappear. It may be objected that whenever a misbehaved member is laughed at or is refused interaction, it is a particular neighbour or set of neighbours that do the ridiculing and ostracising. And that is true. But the deterrent effect of these informal punishments does not depend on the personal identity of those laughing or refusing to interact, and if the deterrent effect can be achieved by any set of neighbours engaging in ridiculing or ostracising, then the effect cannot be reduced to persons.[2]

A different example is provided by institutional organisations like universities, hospitals, factories, churches and government agencies. Unlike communities, these assemblages have an authority structure, in which orders flow down the chain of command while reports (about the outcomes of following orders) flow upwards. Authority can always be imposed through physical punishment or incarceration, but a less costly way is provided by legitimacy. The members of an organisation may believe that commands are legitimate for a variety of reasons, but whatever these are, as long as a critical mass of coworkers share these beliefs they will obey without the need for punishment. In small organisations, like religious sects, the charisma of the leader may ensure the validity of authority, but larger organisations need a legitimising tradition, enshrined in a sacred book and displayed through rituals that preserve a continuity with the past.

Religious and aristocratic organisations are like this. But other organisations, like modern bureaucracies, lack such a traditional basis and must rely on a set of written regulations defining roles, rights and obligations, as well as on the actual performance of their function: if a bureaucratic agency in charge of emergency relief fails to move decisively and efficiently when

Urban Territorialisation and
Deterritorialisation

this spread and overleaf: The territorialisation parameter in terms of urban assemblages tracks the historical process of the dissolution of city boundaries: from walled 15th-century Florence, to 19th-century London opened up by the railway, to 20th-century Los Angeles dissolving into boundless suburbia.

below: Florence, or Catena, *c* 1471–82, attributed to Francesco di Lorenzo Rosselli.

A tightly knit community, such as those we find in small towns or in ethnic neighbourhoods in large cities, is characterised by the fact that every community member knows every other member.

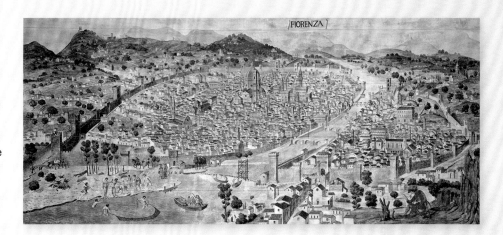

disaster strikes, it will lose legitimacy in the eyes of its members as well as in those of other organisations. The extent to which legitimacy is truly emergent and irreducible varies depending on its source. At one extreme is the charismatic type, which depending as it does on a personal attribute of the leader is clearly not emergent. At the other extreme is a government agency in which resources are linked to an office, not to the incumbent of that office. In this case, legitimacy has become impersonal, and hence fully emergent. The case of traditional legitimacy is intermediary: the weight of the past clearly places constraints on what a leader can do, but there is plenty of room for capricious or arbitrary decisions.[3]

It is important to emphasise that in both cases the working parts of the assemblage are not only of people (neighbours or coworkers), but also of a variety of other inorganic, organic and social components: the neighbourhood houses, and the hospital, university, or agency buildings that shelter the community or organisation; the flows of external matter and energy that keep them alive, as well as the flows of money needed to mobilise those external flows; the tools and machines that are used in the performance of domestic or professional tasks. Adding these other components

is what allows assemblages to capture social entities of intermediate scale in concrete terms. Thus we are never dealing with 'the community' or 'the organisation' in abstract terms, but always with this community in this town, or this organisation in this government in this country. Moreover, since these assemblages are always concretely embodied and spatially situated, it is easy to imagine them forming larger wholes. Cities, in particular, can be viewed as assemblages of many communities and many organisations, as well as of the varied infrastructure needed to interconnect them and facilitate their daily practices. Cities, in turn, can form larger assemblages, such as urban regions made out of towns of different sizes, with the largest town typically serving as a regional capital.[4]

Depending on the speed of transportation, these regions can acquire a variety of emergent forms: the central place hierarchies of landlocked cities that emerged when movement was by foot or horse; the less hierarchical regions that formed around maritime ports engaged in international trade; the string-of-beads pattern promoted by the railroad as new towns grew around stations; and finally, the more dispersed arrangements made possible by the automobile. Once we have conceived of urban regions

below top: Aerial view of London, 1846, showing the general line of the proposed Tottenham and Farringdon Street Extension Railway, from the end of Hatton Garden passing through Clerkenwell, Islington, Stoke Newington and Clapton.

below bottom: Los Angeles, c 1955; cloverleaf freeway interchange and suburban housing developments.

While in the previous century commuters still had to come to the central city to work, shop, and do official business, by the 1950s suburbanites could find all the services they needed outside the city. Cities, in a word, became multi-centred.

as concrete entities we can use them to compose larger provinces, and then use the latter to think about the historical processes through which many provinces were stitched together into countries, processes that in many instances involve military interventions. In all cases, the properties that characterise a whole are emergent, and the components are related in exteriority; that is, linked through relations that are not constitutive of their identity.

However, the concept of assemblage remains incomplete if only emergence and exteriority are considered. In particular, because the identity of each assemblage is historical the degree to which this identity is well defined is bound to change with time, getting sharper or fuzzier depending on a variety of factors. To capture this temporal dimension, we can parametrise the assemblage. A simple way of thinking about this is to take the concept and build into it 'control knobs', the different settings of which determine how well defined the identity of the assemblage is at any given time. Most social assemblages must be equipped with at least two parameters: one determining how rigid or flexible its boundaries are, and how homogeneous or heterogeneous its components are; the other defining the degree to which the identity of the assemblage is constituted and maintained by language.

The first parameter may be said to quantify the degree of territorialisation or deterritorialisation of the assemblage, and the second its degree of coding and decoding. Let us illustrate the effect that turning these parameters in one direction or the other has on the identity of a social assemblage. Imagine a city in which its different neighbourhoods are inhabited by communities of different religions or ethnic backgrounds, and think of a peaceful period of time in its history. At that point, each community will have a low value of the territorialisation parameter: the boundaries of each neighbourhood will not be actively policed and there will typically be regular contact (or even intermarriage) among their members. Then imagine a civil war is triggered by some critical event, forcing communities not only to rigidify the neighbourhood borders (with violent gangs performing the enforcement), but also to police their members more intensely: Are you a real Muslim? A real Christian? A real Jew?

Do you belong to us or to them? Conflict between communities, in short, tends to sharpen their boundaries and to force them to become less tolerant of internal differences.[5] This causes the assemblage to rigidify and homogenise; that is, to increase its degree of territorialisation.

The opposite can be illustrated by the effects that the advent of long-distance communication can have on communities. As far back as the 17th century, dispersed communities of scientists existed in which the ties that bound them were maintained through regular correspondence. This, of course, presupposed a certain infrastructure (a reliable postal service) and the performance of specialised labour: scientific communities had to have multilingual members dedicated to reading and answering letters. Since the members of these communities did not inhabit the same geographical location, the community's borders were not at all well defined. To be sure, many members congregated in cities that were centres of research (Paris, London, Berlin), but even these members did not live in physical proximity to each other. Despite this geographical dispersion, however, scientific communities had emergent capacities – ridicule and ostracism were still effective weapons against fraud and unbridled speculation – even if these were somewhat weaker. The advent of more powerful communication technologies, such as the Internet, has created the conditions for a more thorough deterritorialisation of these assemblages, many of which do not have any definite boundaries. And although many of these 'virtual communities' form around common interests, they can also be tolerant of differences or even thrive on heterogeneity as a source of inspiration.

The territorialisation parameter can also be used to characterise the different conditions in which social assemblages exist at different times in their history. For example, the spatial boundaries of most medieval cities were sharply defined by their defensive walls. The land on which these cities rose was usually owned by a feudal lord, but in several parts of Europe city-states had managed to rent it from its owners. However, the extent of their contractual autonomy extended only to the limit marked by their walls, as did the jurisdiction of the local authorities. These cities can be said to have existed in a highly territorialised condition. After the Thirty Years' War,

when many cities were absorbed by larger countries, defensive walls became part of the frontiers of kingdoms and empires, while the cities in their interiors lost this defining feature. In the 19th century, the railroad made possible the creation of residential suburbs, and as these began changing the journey to work (commuting) their borders became even fuzzier. Finally, with the advent of the automobile and of suburbs that offered the same differentiation of land uses as the central city (residential, industrial, governmental, retail) the borders of cities became fully deterritorialised: while in the previous century commuters still had to come to the central city to work, shop, and do official business, by the 1950s suburbanites could find all the services they needed outside the city. Cities, in a word, became multi-centred.[6]

To illustrate the second parameter we can begin with social practices that are entirely defined by language, such as playing a game of chess. The identity of chess pieces and their possible interactions are constituted by the rules of chess, so we may consider the assemblage formed by two players, two sets of pieces and a chequerboard as a highly coded assemblage. But a better example are communities or organisations in which specific speech-acts (not just a set of linguistic statements) create social obligations binding the members: a promise, a command, a marriage vow, a judge's sentence. A highly coded assemblage in this case would be represented by a military organisation in which orders from above determine the behaviour of those below, and in which all rights and obligations are spelt out in a book of regulations. Government bureaucracies, large industrial corporations and religious organisations like the Vatican rely on a rigid command structure, a state that can be captured by setting the coding parameter of these assemblages to a high value. On the other hand, prices, when they are set impersonally by demand and supply, transmit information about the latter that can be used to make decentralised decisions about buying and selling. Organisations that, like bazaars, use prices as the main form of coordination of social activities may be said to be decoded (and prices themselves to have a decoding effect). In this case too we often find mixtures: many large firms use prices to manage their costs, but then add a markup as a command to determine

the final price, a combination that can be captured by an intermediate value of the coding parameter.

The value of parametrising the concept of assemblage becomes clearer when we consider that in most cases the components of a social assemblage are themselves assemblages: industrial networks (such as the network of suppliers and distributors linked to a large firm like General Motors) are assemblages of organisations, each of which is an assemblage of people. Hence, when exploring the history of a particular industry we need to be able to locate at what level of the part-to-whole relation a deterritorialisation or decoding effect has occurred. We can, of course, simply follow tradition and fuse all these assemblages into a seamless totality, the capitalist system, and go on to speculate about 'the laws' of this macro entity. But if we do that we completely lose track of all the important historical events occurring at the meso-scale: the differences between landlocked cities trading in local goods and maritime cities engaged in international trade in luxury goods; the differences between an oligopoly of three or four dominant companies and a network of hundreds of small firms competing in terms of design not costs; the differences between a large public corporation run by managers and a small private business run by an entrepreneur. In order to increase the resolution of our historical analyses, in order to be able to discern all the differences that make a difference, we need to conceptually build the meso-scale one layer at a time. A parametrised concept of wholes that are both irreducible and decomposable, a concept that can be used recursively, is precisely what we need for such an important task. ⌀

Notes
1. Manuel DeLanda, *A New Philosophy of Society*, Continuum (London), 2005, pp 9–11.
2. *Ibid.* pp 56–8.
3. Max Weber, *The Theory of Social and Economic Organization*, Free Press of Glencoe (New York), 1964, pp 328–60.
4. Paul M Hohenberg and Lynn Hollen Lees, *The Making of Urban Europe 1000–1950*, Harvard University Press (Cambridge, MA), 1985, ch 2.
5. Graham Crow, *Social Solidarities*, Open University Press (Buckingham), 2002, pp 128–9.
6. James E Vance Jr, *The Continuing City: Urban Morphology in Western Civilization*, John Hopkins University Press (Baltimore, MD), 1990, ch 8.

A Hospice for Parametricism

COUNTERPOINT
02/2016
No 240
AD

Could Parametricism 2.0 prove the final resting place for Parametricism 1.0? Architect and Assistant Dean of the Yale School of Architecture, **Mark Foster Gage** questions the underlying currency and influence of Parametricism, condemning it as a 'true red herring' of a style.

Biblia Ingentis Magnitudinis

Patrik Schumacher's Parametricism manifesto, presented in his two-volume set *The Autopoiesis of Architecture* (2011–12), weighs in at nearly 1,200 pages.[1] For reference, my family's *King James Bible*, including both the Old and New Testaments, weighs in at a mere 922. With nearly 30 per cent more to say than God, Patrik is a rare and terrifying occurrence in academia – a true believer, a fanatic even, as perhaps best described by fellow Londoner Winston Churchill as 'one who can't change his mind and won't change the subject'. Which brings us rather fittingly to the subject at hand, not only Parametricism – but *more* Parametricism; this round labelled, creatively, as 'Parametricism 2.0'. It stands to reason that any successes to be found in this rerelease, or reboot, as Parametricism 2.0 must inherently build on those of Parametricism 1.0. The question is – were there any?

Any discussion of Parametricism, regardless of the release number, needs to begin with Schumacher's aforementioned Bible-dwarfing *Autopoiesis of Architecture* texts. To understand these books, however, it might be prudent to start with a somewhat lighter reference – David Cross's book *I Drink for a Reason* (2009), which not only seems apt for yet another discussion on Parametricism, but also features on its back cover the tart quip by the actor Paul Rudd and future parametrically scaled *Ant-Man* who claims it to be: 'One of the funniest books I've ever skimmed!!!'[2] Schumacher's 'magnum opus' (Latin translation: 'great work', his words),[3] *The Autopoiesis of Architecture* is, likewise, best skimmed, as it is, at least for me, and as with a great deal of architectural theory, unnecessarily lengthy and, in significant stretches, indecipherable – prompting Steve Parnell of the *Architects' Journal* to review it as 'surely the longest and, quite possibly, the most opaque manifesto in architectural historiography'.[4] And yet, despite its Maherian 'religulous'[5] length, frequently twisted jargon, intellectual hiccups and downright antique militant-manifesto tone, it is nearly solely responsible for introducing the hotly contested topic of what one can only call 'Schumacherian Parametricism' into the discourse of architecture – no small feat in a discipline flooded with the post-starchitect allergy to monolithic disciplinary claims. This is commendable, and if it were not based on content but length alone, it might even have, as recalled by Peter Buchanan, met the expectations that Schumacher had of his book on Parametricism at its launch – that it 'was going to eclipse anything since Le Corbusier's "Vers Une Architecture"'.[6] It didn't. Nor did it become, again in Schumacher's own words, 'The great new style after Modernism'.[7]

Mark Foster Gage Architects, House on Ile René-Lavasseur, Manicouagan Crater Lake, Quebec, 2015

This project further developed the language of kitbashing through increased levels of abstraction from the original referents, which further disempowered the legibility of the original part-derived formal relationships.

Parametricism Is Not and Has Never Been a Style

Instead, Parametricism 1.0, like Microsoft's Zune, never really caught on as an intellectual idea in the profession or discipline outside the Architectural Association (AA) in London and other areas of Schumacher's direct personal influence – for reasons we will get to shortly. Schumacher acknowledges this when he describes the manifesto for the book you now hold in your hand, stating: 'The aim of this issue of $\mathcal{D}$ is to try to halt and reverse the increasing marginalisation of Parametricism' (see p 9). This marginalisation of Parametricism is not in dispute – it is on life support, having been held together too long by the unlikely cocktail of AA students, pop-tart-fuelled scripters and a touch of megalomania. I would go so far as to suggest that had the idea of a 'parametric style' come from anyone other than the partner of global architectural powerhouse Zaha Hadid, Parametricism 1.0 as a stylistic idea, much less 'the great new style after Modernism', would have gone nearly entirely unnoticed in the marketplace of architectural ideas. This is because 'Schumacherian Parametricism' is neither a style nor a movement, but merely a now ubiquitous 21st-century technology coupled with a stylistic preference for topologically derived (smooth) digital surfaces – an aesthetic to which, in the interest of full disclosure, I also have affinities. Parametricism as a technology, however, inherently has no style, and can be used to support any number of 'styles'. There is no reason that a Tuscan-style suburban house cannot be technologically parametric – in fact, because of various building information modelling (BIM) technologies, most already are.

This is one key fault in Schumacher's claims of Parametricism as a style; that it relies on a tenuous link between mostly smooth, 'continuously differentiated' digital surfaces and contemporary parametric technologies. If one doubts the purely formal and aesthetic foundations of Schumacher's smooth parametric style, consider the formal nature of the decreed 'rules' that Parametricist architecture must obey; that it has 'no platonic, discrete figures with sharp outlines', and that one must 'avoid familiar typologies, avoid platonic/hermetic objects, avoid clear-cut zones/territories, avoid repetition, avoid straight lines, avoid right angles, avoid corners …'.[8] Mario Carpo, in his 'Parametric Notations: The Birth of the Non-Standard' on pp 24–9 of this issue, takes this observation to its logical extreme and writes: 'the logic of digital Parametricism has changed, or is poised to change, the way we make almost everything – and, together with the technical basis of our civilisation, it has already changed the world in which we live.'

To be architecturally parametric is to have emerged from parameters that influence agents, measurements or components, as opposed to having been more wilfully composed with forms. While certainly supercharged by digital technologies, Parametricism is not particularly new to the discipline of architecture. Classicism is, in fact, entirely parametric in its use of measure and geometry. The designs of significant buildings, as far back as and preceding the Temple of Hera at Olympia (590 BC), were generated via intricately proliferating fractional dimensions based on the diameter of a column. If the diameter of the column, and therefore the column spacing and building scale, changed, all additional components from the stylobate to the most minute guttae would require a change in design. That is to say if one single parameter changed, the whole building had to update accordingly. The majority of Vitruvius's *Ten Books on Architecture*, published in the first century BC and the only full text on architecture to survive from antiquity, along with Leon Battista Alberti's own Ten Books, *De Re Aedificatoria*, its Renaissance descendant written in 1452 (and the point where Schumacher claims architecture actually begins), are largely recipe books of these parameters that intricately and algorithmically link components to each other proportionally in order to produce predictable yet variable wholes. Contemporary architecture has a monopoly on neither complexity nor Parametricism. Mark Burry, in his text in this issue (pp 30–35), similarly notes, using more recent precedents, that 'The significance of the similarities between Gaudí and Otto as predigital precursors for designing parametrically counters any claim that Parametricism, in itself, is merely a contemporary digital condition'. So if Parametricism was already present in architectural history from antiquity through to the 20th century, and is omnipresent in contemporary society as Carpo suggests, why are bikini-waxed fluid digital surfaces so absolutely required for Parametricism's formal manifestation in architecture today?

Mark Foster Gage Architects, Helsinki Guggenheim Museum proposal, Helsinki, 2014

The project pioneered a language of architectural 'kitbashing' as a manifestation of Bruno Latour's 'litanies' and similar anti-narrative philosophical devices used by contemporary philosopher Graham Harman in his writings on 'object-oriented ontology'.

The true red herring of Parametricism as a style, that nobody seems to want to address, is that through brilliant design virtuosity and impeccable timing, Zaha Hadid has absorbed the language of digital, supple, continuous surfaces as an extension of her historically fluid signature – rendering it dangerous territory for use by most, and certainly most emerging, architects who seek to develop their own pathways in the profession – as opposed to working with derivatives of someone else's. This likely accounts for Schumacher's statement in his Introduction to this issue (pp 8–17) that evidence of this marginalisation of Parametricism 'is apparent in its fading influence within schools of architecture'. That is to say that the 'style' of Parametricism is not something with a lot of mileage left for other architects, as it is not really, as we have determined, a parametric style as much as a smoothly surfaced style, and therefore one simply recognised globally, and likely historically, as 'Zaha Hadid's

style'. Schumacher's references to Parametricism replacing both Le Corbusier's *Vers Une Architecture* and the International Style are the wrong historical model. I would suggest that the gorgeous fluid signature of Hadid, being so recognisably her own, is much closer to a historical model of Frank Lloyd Wright – an absolute master whose signature is so author-specific as to be nearly untouchable by other architects. In this light, Schumacherian Parametricism is destined not to become the next great global style as much as the new Taliesin – a school of thought with very few, but very dedicated – nay fanatical – believers content to rehearse old architectural scripts well beyond their expiration date. Parametricism 2.0 will, at best, function as a siren song to attract such a constituency, because to otherwise insist that students or architects today have any desire to mimic the great masters, Hadid included, is a gross misreading of both the state of the architectural landscape and the value placed on individuality in our selfie-dominated today.

Snooze, More Deleuze

As if all this were not enough to lay Parametricism to rest, its disciplinary shortcomings are also perfumed with the scent of decaying philosophical stagnation. The Deleuzian philosophical basis for Schumacher's parametric style is simply out of steam, having been the basis for over a quarter of a century of architectural speculation. Carpo addresses this origin when he writes in his article that: 'Digital Parametricism, as we know it today, was born on page 26 of the first edition of Gilles Deleuze's book *The Fold*, first published in French in 1988' (p 26). The Schumacherian parametric project, 28 years later, is perhaps simultaneously the greatest achievement, and last gasp, of a strong Deleuzian influence in architectural discourse. Perhaps the time has come to move beyond all things folded, vague, nomadic, smoothly differentiated and in an ever-perpetuating state of becoming but never arriving. A new school of thought in architecture, or what some might have called a new avant-garde were the very concept not so quaint, seems to be rising to fill the vacuum left over from this Deleuzian/parametric end game. The impetus for this shift largely emerges not from Schumacher's worries about architectural 'anti-iconicity' and 'Neo-Rationalism', but from a far more powerful shift in the underlying framework of contemporary philosophy.

A new generation of architects today, many battle-scarred from fighting to advance the use of the technologies, but certainly not the discourse, that Schumacher is claiming ownership of, is being re-energised by a direct association with realist philosopher and Professor and Associate Vice Provost for Research at the American University in Cairo, Graham Harman, who through his increasingly influential philosophy of 'object-oriented ontology' (OOO) offers a bold challenge to the 'linguistic turn' and idealism basis of Western philosophy so increasingly dominant since the Enlightenment. The reason OOO is being explored by these architects is that it functions as an antidote not only to the Deleuzian emphasis on becoming over being, but, by extension, to architecture being justified not by its own qualities, but by its relations – its process, its internal complexity, its contextual relations, its LEED certification – or by its parametric origins or status.[9] The reframed philosophical context of OOO challenges, in particular, Deleuzian-cum-Schumacherian Parametricism in which all parameters are constantly shifting, but ultimately known, interconnected, procedural and calculable, and offers the possibility of an architecture of less predictable experiential outcomes, rather than one of forced obedience to the social and communicatory scripts outlined by the architect. In such an architecture, qualities are not necessarily all foreseen or traceable, and far less importance is placed on relationships in favour of a greater role for independent entities (no, not object buildings). Harman has in fact thoroughly outlined these positions and lectured extensively against Schumacher's Parametricist position in numerous school of architecture – most forcefully in September 2013 at the Southern California Institute of Architecture (SCI-Arc) in a lecture entitled, rather specifically, 'Strange Objects: *Contra Parametricism*'.

Mark Foster Gage Architects,
57th Street Tower, New York
City, New York, 2015

top: The 57th Street tower project
experimented with new forms of
'continuous differentiation' that derive
not from the repetition and variation
of primitives as found in early digital
formalism or Schumacherian Parametricism,
but rather collisions of unrelated yet highly
detailed objects that are composed through
scale, orientation and material effects into
perplexingly cohesive new wholes.

Mark Foster Gage, 'Disheveled
Geometries: Kitbashing'
research seminar, Yale
University, New Haven,
Connecticut, 2014

bottom: The image illustrates the 'sensual'
and perceivable effects of kitbashing-made
material revealed through variations in
lighting. The research was completed
in association with Autodesk, with a
large 3D-printed kitbashed model from
Materialise. Graduate student participants
included: Adam Wagoner, Madelynn Ringo,
Daniel Nguyen, Peter Le, Evira Hoxha, Emily
Bell, Dionysus Cho, Jack Wolfe, Anne Ma
and Junpei Okai.

Notes

1. Patrik Schumacher, *The Autopoiesis of
Architecture, Vols I and II*, John Wiley & Sons
(Chichester), 2011 and 2012.
2. David Cross, *I Drink for a Reason*, Grand
Central Publishers (New York), 2009, back
cover.
3. See Schumacher's personal website
where he states: 'After 10 years of focused
theoretical work I am happy to finally
announce the forthcoming publication
of my theoretical "opus magnum".'
www.patrikschumacher.com/Texts/
Announcement_The%20Autopoeisis%20
of%20Architecture.html.
4. Steven Parnell, 'The Style War Continues',
Architects' Journal, 17 February 2011:
www.architectsjournal.co.uk/the-style-war-
continues/8611435.article.
5. To better understand the reference, see
Bill Maher's movie *Religulous*, Icon Films,
2008.
6. Peter Buchanan, 'The Autopoeisis of
Architecture: Dissected, Discussed and
Decoded', *Architectural Review*, March 2011.
7. See the transcript of Schumacher's lecture
'Parametricism as Style – Parametricist
Manifesto', delivered originally at the
Dark Side Club, 11th Venice Architecture
Biennale, 2008, on his website:
www.patrikschumacher.com/Texts/
Parametricism%20as%20Style.htm.
8. *Ibid*.
9. For more information on object-oriented
ontology in architecture, see Mark Foster
Gage, 'Killing Simplicity: Object Oriented
Ontology in Architecture', *Log 33*, Winter
2014, pp 95–106.
10. Patrik Schumacher, 'Convergence Versus
Fragmentation', *Fulcrum*, 19, 10 June 2011,
p 1.
11. Graham Harman, *Bells and Whistles:
More Speculative Realism*, Zero Books
(Winchester), 2013, p 100.
12. Patrik Schumacher, *The Autopoiesis
of Architecture, Vol I: A New Framework
for Architecture*, John Wiley & Sons
(Chichester), 2011, p 277.

The Last Supper

In 2011, Robert AM Stern organised a small dinner at Philip Johnson's Four Seasons restaurant in New York that included, among a few others, Zaha Hadid, Peter Eisenman, Patrik Schumacher and myself. Bob Stern, with characteristic mischievousness and expecting fireworks, sat Patrik and I next to each other knowing, as he did, of our recent heated disagreements regarding Parametricism (1.0) in the AA publication *Fulcrum* where Schumacher had written about me such niceties as 'to shy away from taking a principled position, is a sign of impotence'.[10] Patrik and I have, entirely as friends, been slapping each other with lilies regarding the topic of Parametricism for nearly half a decade at this point, and I feel the need to note prior to the imminent collapse of Parametricism as a 'style' that I have a profound respect for what Zaha and Patrik have achieved professionally and, especially for Patrik, given that in his 'free time' between teaching and co-running a world-class architecture firm, he has managed to dedicate such resources to architectural thinking. It is unfortunate that such epic documentation was dedicated to a line of thinking with such little mileage left. Schumacher's predictable obsessions with communicatory relations, complexity, and networked agents and fields are entirely understandable as such topics are all aspects of the great master narrative of the last quarter century – interconnectedness. Regarding this, Harman writes: 'Every event in the contemporary world seems to sing the praises of interconnectivity: globalization convergence, super powerful communications media and the new cosmopolitanism, along with the nested feedback loops of climate change.'[11] Like James Cameron's *Avatar* (2009), we have all been sold on the idea that we, and everything, are all connected, always – and that it is the communicative relationships between things that define them rather than the entities (in Harmanian terms 'objects') themselves being the real material of reality. The time has come to take a new in-depth look at the actual qualities of entities that surround us and not ignore their existence in favour of their stories – in most cases, the same old story of interconnectedness. In a world where everything is already interconnected it is no longer a progressive position to insist the future lies in interconnectivity – whether it be of the Avatarian/ecological or the Schumacherian communicatory-social-parametric variety.

In the introduction to this issue, Schumacher frequently rephrases this predictable and exhausted worldview through summarising the views of his contributors, such as Theodore Spyropoulos, who he says 'conceives architecture as an ecology of interacting systems'. Schumacher himself states in this same introduction that: 'Only Parametricism can adequately organise and articulate contemporary social assemblages at the level of complexity called for today' (p 17). OOO proposes a philosophical basis that reframes architecture not as contingent on orchestrated communicative relations, but rather invested in the production of sensible/sensual, slippery and inferrable architectural qualities independent of their narrative relations. Schumacher mistakes recent attacks on Parametricism as emerging only from 'anti-iconicity' and 'Neo-Rationalist' camps, but its true downfall is being brought about not from an assault on its frivolity as much as on its formal and philosophical conservativeness. He has actually penned his own self-fulfilling biblical Revelations prophecy for the endgame, or rapture, of Parametricism as a style as the '16th thesis' from his own *Autopoiesis of Architecture* where he writes: 'Avant-garde styles are design research programmes. They start as progressive research programmes, mature to become productive dogmas, and end as degenerate dogmas.'[12] It is the degenerate dogmas that should, albeit with dignity and compassion, and surrounded by friends and gently used lilies, be allowed to die in peace. ⌂

Shajay Bhooshan is an associate at Zaha Hadid Architects in London where he heads the computation and design group (ZHACODE). He is also a studio master in the Architectural Association Design Research Laboratory (AADRL) master's programme. He is an MPhil candidate at the University of Bath, and a Research Fellow at the Institute of Technology in Architecture, ETH Zurich, where he was part of the Block Research Group (BRG). He previously worked at Populous, London, and completed his Master's degree at the AADRL in 2006.

Philippe Block is Associate Professor at the Institute of Technology in Architecture, ETH Zurich, where he codirects the Block Research Group (BRG) with Dr Tom Van Mele, focusing on graphical and computational form-finding, optimisation and fabrication of curved surface structures. He studied architecture and structural engineering at the Vrije Universiteit Brussel and received his PhD from the Massachusetts Institute of Technology (MIT) in 2009. With Ochsendorf DeJong & Block, LLC (ODB), he applies his research into practice on the structural assessment of historic monuments in unreinforced masonry and the design and engineering of compression structures.

Mark Burry is a practising architect, and has published on Antoni Gaudí, and on putting theory into practice with 'challenging' architecture. He is Senior Architect to the Sagrada Família Basilica Foundation, pioneering distant collaboration with his Barcelona colleagues. In December 2014 he joined the University of Melbourne as Professor of Urban Futures at the Faculty of Architecture, Building and Planning, where he will further develop the faculty's capacity to consolidate research in urban futures, drawing together expertise in urban visualisation, analytics and policy. Prior to this appointment, he was the Founding Director of RMIT University's Design Research Institute (DRI) and also founded the university's state-of-the-art Spatial Information Architecture Laboratory (SIAL).

Mario Carpo is Reyner Banham Professor of Architectural Theory and History at the Bartlett School of Architecture, University College London (UCL). His research and publications focus on the relationship between architectural theory, cultural history, and the history of media and information technology. His *Architecture in the Age of Printing* (MIT Press, 2001) has been translated into several languages. His most recent books are *The Alphabet and the Algorithm* (MIT Press, 2011), a history of digital design theory; and *The Digital Turn in Architecture, 1992–2012* (John Wiley & Sons, 2013).

Manuel DeLanda is an artist and philosopher. He is faculty and a Professor of Graduate Architecture and Urban Design (GAUD) at Pratt Institute, New York. He is the author of seven philosophy books: *War in the Age of Intelligent Machines* (Zone Books, 1991), *A Thousand Years of Nonlinear History* (Zone Books, 1997), *Intensive Science and Virtual Philosophy* (Athlone, 2002), *A New Philosophy of Society* (Continuum, 2006), *Deleuze: History and Science* (Atropos, 2010), *Philosophy and Simulation* (Continuum, 2011) and *Philosophical Chemistry* (Bloomsbury, 2015).

Marc Fornes is a registered and practising architect. He is also a fine connoisseur in computer science, investigating design through codes and computational protocols. Produced under his label THEVERYMANY™ his extensive body of research – addressing ways to describe complex curvilinear self-supported surfaces into series of flat elements – is constantly reinventing the field of computational skinning. As THEVERYMANY, Fornes has designed and installed temporary and permanent installations around the world. His projects are part of the permanent collections of several museums, including the Centre Pompidou, and have been exhibited at the Guggenheim Museum in New York and GGG Art Basel Miami.

John Frazer is a leader in the field of generative design and evolutionary computation. He was the inventor of tangible interfaces and the originator of the Evolutionary Digital Design Process. His research at Cambridge University and the AA has been extensively published, and his book *An Evolutionary Architecture* (AA Publications, 1995) is the seminal work in the discipline. He is currently a Professor at the European Graduate School and Chair of the Frazer Foundation for Accelerating Architecture.

Mark Foster Gage is the founder of Mark Foster Gage Architects LLC in New York, as well as the Assistant Dean of the Yale School of Architecture. He has written extensively on design and philosophy in academic publications including *⚙D*, *JAE*, *Volume*, *Fulcrum*, *Perspecta* and *LOG*, for which he also guest co-edited issue #19. His design work has been exhibited in institutions including the Museum of Modern Art (MoMA), New York, and the Museum of the Art Institute of Chicago, as well as featured in the media in locations including *Vogue*, the *New York Times*, *Harper's Bazaar* and MTV.

Enriqueta Llabres is the founder of London-based Relational Urbanism, a multidisciplinary office practising landscape, architecture and urbanism that focuses on cultural and design solutions to social, environmental and development issues. She gained her MSc in Local Economic Development from the London School of Economics (LSE), and is currently a teaching fellow in design at the Bartlett School of Architecture, UCL, and a lecturer in landscape architecture at Harvard University Graduate School of Design (GSD).

Achim Menges is a registered architect and professor at the University of Stuttgart, where he is the founding director of the Institute for Computational Design. He also is Visiting Professor in Architecture at Harvard GSD. His work has received international attention for its innovative take on fusing computation and materialisation in architecture. It has won numerous international awards, and been published and exhibited worldwide.

Ross Lovegrove is a designer and visionary whose work is considered to be at the very apex of stimulating a profound change in the physicality of our three-dimensional world. Inspired by the logic and beauty of nature his designs possess a trinity between technology, materials science and intelligent organic form, creating what many industrial leaders see as the new aesthetic expression for the 21st century. There is always embedded a deeply human and resourceful approach in his designs, which project an optimism and innovative vitality in everything he touches from cameras to cars to trains, aviation and architecture.

Eduardo Rico is a civil engineer and MA Landscape Urbanism graduate, and part of the Arup infrastructure design team. He codirects the academic and research agendas of Relational Urbanism, and is also Director of the MA Landscape Urbanism at the AA in London. He has collaborated with Groundlab in projects such as Longang masterplan and Xian Flowing Gardens, and has also taught at the Berlage, Bartlett School of Architecture, UCL and Harvard GSD.

Theodore Spyropoulos is an architect and educator. He is the Director of the Architectural Association Design Research Lab (AADRL) in London. He has been a visiting Research Fellow at MIT's Center for Advanced Visual Studies (CAVS), and has taught at the graduate schools of the University of Pennsylvania (Upenn), Royal College of Art (RCA) and University of Innsbruck. In 2002 he founded the experimental architecture and design practice Minimaforms. The practice's work has been acquired by the collections of the FRAC Centre, Orléans, the Signum Foundation and the Archigram Archive. He has exhibited at MoMA, New York, the Barbican Centre and Institute of Contemporary Arts (ICA) in London, and the Detroit Institute of Arts (DIA). His published books include *Adaptive Ecologies: Correlated Systems of Living* (AA Publications, 2013) and *Enabling: The Work of Minimaforms* (AA Publications, 2010).

Robert Stuart-Smith is the director of architectural practice Robert Stuart-Smith Design, a co-founding director of research practice Kokkugia, and a Studio Course Master at the AADRL. Robert Stuart-Smith Design was the recipient of the 2014 RCA Design Innovation Award, and is currently working on projects in the UK, Indonesia, Greece and Australia. Stuart-Smith's work has been widely published and exhibited, is in the permanent collection of the FRAC Centre, and has received multiple nominations for Russia's Chernikhov Prize. He has lectured internationally at institutions including the MIT Media Lab, ICD at the University of Stuttgart, ETH Zurich, and University of Applied Arts Vienna.

Philip F Yuan is an Associate Professor in Architecture at Tongji University in Shanghai, and the director of the Digital Design Research Center (DDRC) at the College of Architecture and Urban Planning (CAUP), Tongji University. He is also the founding director of Archi-Union Architects. As one of the founders of the Digital Architectural Design Association (DADA) of the Architectural Society of China (ASC), his research and practice focuses on digital design and fabrication methodology with the combination of Chinese traditional material and craftsmanship. His research publications include *A Tectonic Reality* (China Architecture & Building Press, 2011), as well as *Theater Design* (2012), *Fabricating the Future* (2012), *Scripting the Future* (2012), *Digital Workshop in China* (2013) and *Robotic Futures* (2015), all published by Tongji University Press.

What is Architectural Design?

Founded in 1930, *Architectural Design* (△) is an influential and prestigious publication. It combines the currency and topicality of a newsstand journal with the rigour and production qualities of a book. With an almost unrivalled reputation worldwide, it is consistently at the forefront of cultural thought and design.

Each title of △ is edited by an invited Guest-Editor, who is an international expert in the field. Renowned for being at the leading edge of design and new technologies, △ also covers themes as diverse as architectural history, the environment, interior design, landscape architecture and urban design.

Provocative and inspirational, △ inspires theoretical, creative and technological advances. It questions the outcome of technical innovations as well as the far-reaching social, cultural and environmental challenges that present themselves today.

For further information on △, subscriptions and purchasing single issues see:

www.architectural-design-magazine.com

Volume 85 No 2
ISBN 978 1118 700570

Volume 85 No 3
ISBN 978 1118 829011

Volume 85 No 4
ISBN 978 1118 914830

Volume 85 No 5
ISBN 978 1118 878378

Volume 85 No 6
ISBN 978 1118 915646

Volume 86 No 1
ISBN 978 1118 910641

How to Subscribe
With 6 issues a year, you can subscribe to △ (either print, online or through the △ App for iPad)

Institutional subscription
£212 / US$398 print or online

Institutional subscription
£244 / US$457 combined print and online

Personal-rate subscription
£120 / US$189 print and iPad access

Student-rate subscription
£75 / US$117 print only

△ App for iPad
6-issue subscription:
£44.99 / US$64.99
Individual issue:
£9.99 / US$13.99

To subscribe to print or online
E: cs-journals@wiley.com

Americas
E: cs-journals@wiley.com
T: +1 781 388 8598
or +1 800 835 6770
(toll free in the USA & Canada)

Europe, Middle East and Africa
E: cs-journals@wiley.com
T: +44 (0) 1865 778315

Asia Pacific
E: cs-journals@wiley.com
T: +65 6511 8000

Japan (for Japanese-speaking support)
E: cs-japan@wiley.com
T: +65 6511 8010
or 005 316 50 480
(toll-free)

Visit our Online Customer Help available in 7 languages at www.wileycustomerhelp.com/ask